Bernadette Wörndl

VIENNESE
Bakery

For
Therese & Maria

Bernadette
Wörndl

VIENNESE
Bakery

Classic desserts from
Vienna's café culture

With photographs by
Melina Kutelas

Contents

Preface

Therese Schulz was born near Vienna in 1884 as one of seven children. While still a young adult, she became the bakery manager at the luxurious Grand Hotel on Vienna's Ringstrasse, a place frequented by nobility, celebrities, politicians, and artists.

She always carried with her a hand-written booklet in which she kept a neat record of all the secret recipes and favorite bakeries that were particularly popular. The booklet of original recipes was eventually passed on to her niece, who in turn handed down this precious text to Therese's great-great-niece, Eva Scheiringer.

I own a recipe booklet of this kind too—it belonged to my grandmother Maria, and I guard it like a treasure. That's why I was immediately inspired by the idea of bringing the Viennese Bakery of the last century into the present. But before this was possible, I had to become a kind of translator between these different eras.

Therese recorded all her favorite recipes in an old form of German cursive handwriting, and the preferred unit of measurement was the Loth (a historical measure used in Austria until the late 19th century). Information such as "one Seidel *of wine" or "a thought of cinnamon" also had to be converted into more modern units. The ratio of butter, eggs, and sugar was often out of keeping with today's standards, so I adjusted these to more contemporary proportions where that felt appropriate.*

Despite these necessary adjustments, I hope I have managed to stay true to the spirit of Therese in Viennese Bakery.

I certainly feel a close connection to these strong women from previous generations—my grandma, with whom I had the pleasure of spending so much time, and Therese, whose little book I have come to cherish. Thank you for allowing me to convey your recipes into the future.

Bernadette Wörndl

Welcome to 1920s Vienna!

The air is infused with a beguiling floral scent, and there is a pleasant warmth and mild spring breeze. The first violets, primroses, and anemones are poking their heads out of the earth. It's a picture-perfect day. In the gardens of the Schönbrunn Palace, people walk along the crunching gravel paths as they enjoy this springlike Sunday. Among them are sisters Therese and Cilli, who are just walking up the steep slope to the Gloriette monument. From there, the view over the city is heavenly. The sisters are in high spirits. They zigzag back down the path to the palace and hail a carriage. The driver is delighted to get a trip into town, and with such charming passengers too.

Their route takes them along the Vienna River to Karlsplatz, where the golden dome atop the Secession building sparkles in the sunlight. They continue along Ringstrasse, passing first the opera, then the Hofburg and Burggarten on the right. At the Burgtheater, the sisters jump out of their open carriage and walk to the renowned Café Demel. Inside, the room vibrates with the voices of guests, who have all come to nibble on sweet treats. The sisters manage to find themselves a space by the window, where they can be seen in their new spring clothes by passers-by. Dark blue for the understated Therese; pink and violet for the playful Cilli.

From the back of the venue, the melodies of a piano player can be heard, the sound floating through the room like the blossom whirled by the wind outside.

We might picture Therese ordering a small coffee and a slice of Sachertorte (see p.64), while Cilli is tempted to indulge in a Kardinalschnitte (see p.93) and a mocha. Laughter and murmured conversations can be heard in the background. At the neighboring table, a well-known writer scribbles on loose, scattered sheets, while two little girls with neatly braided hair and sailor's clothes play hide-and-seek among the velvet chairs, newspaper stands, and the feet of a gracious young lady. This does little to improve the mood of the head waiter, who is balancing large silver trays with *Melange* (Viennese coffee) and glasses of water as he navigates the room.

Therese (center) with her sisters Cilli (right) and Betti (left).

As usual, the sisters' conversation revolves around their shared passion: baking. From her role at the Grand Hotel am Ring, Therese is familiar with the habits of the great and the good, and always knows which cakes and pastries are fashionable at any moment. Cilli reflects on the many industrious but fun hours spent in the family kitchen. She recalls how—after hours of work—a Dobos Torte (see p.56) slipped out of her hands and landed on the tiles of the kitchen floor. The sisters then ended up baking, layering, and decorating together all through the night to make sure the cake buffet was perfect for the christening of their youngest niece the following day.

Outside the café, the group at the neighboring table leaves, and their place is taken by a distinguished woman. She wears an elegant tailored outfit adorned with lace and ruffles, with a hat perched on her head. Before she even places an order, the head waiter greets her with the words: "My compliments, Miss Wanda," and serves her a perfectly crafted vanilla custard with whipped cream.

Therese is inspired. She quickly takes out a notebook that she always carries with her, lays it on the marble table, and jots down the idea for a new recipe. Delicate, crisp puff pastry with a soft and silky vanilla cream, layered for maximum indulgence, and dusted with powdered sugar to finish. Alongside, she writes "*Miss Wanda Schnitten*" (Miss Wanda's Cream Slice, see p.80).

We cannot know whether this spring day unfolded in the way just described. But the sisters, Therese and Cilli, really did exist, and Therese's notebook is also real. It has remained a well-kept family treasure to this day and—a hundred years later—is a source of inspiration for this book, *Viennese Bakery*.

Pester Schnitten.

Zuckerteig von 15 deka Mehl 14 deka
Butter, 14 deka Zucker, 3 Dotter, ein Brett
anmachen, ein Blech backen, noch warm
in Streifen schneiden mit Chocoladecreme
gefüllt, obenauf anzuckern und bräunen

Esterhazi Schnitten

Loth Zucker in 8 Eiweiß Schnee einschlagen
Loth gebrannte Grillagemandeln, mischen
ein Blech backen, in Streifen schneiden,
mit Buttercreme gefüllt weiß überziehen
von Chocolade ein Gitter spritzen.

Miss Wanda Schnitten.

Von Butterteig Streifen gebacken, mit Rum-
creme füllen, obenauf dann mit weißer
Glasur überzogen mit halbierten weißen
Mandeln bestreuen.

Vienna's architecture—with its decorative facades and imposing columns—and manicured topiary are echoed in the elaborate designs of the city's traditional cakes and patisserie.

Cakes & Tarts

When it's time for coffee and cake in Vienna, classics such as Marmorgugelhupf (see p.18), Rehrücken (see p.28), and Linzer Torte (see p.52) can be found in the lavishly stocked display cases of the city's coffee houses to get the afternoon off to a sweet start.

Marmorgugelhupf

This renowned marble bundt cake is an indispensable accompaniment to afternoon coffee in Vienna. Kaiser Franz Joseph I would have heartily agreed. He was a huge fan of bundt cakes, and even had this exquisite cake served for breakfast.

For 1 bundt cake

FOR THE CAKE

200g unsalted butter, at room temperature, plus extra for greasing
200g powdered sugar, plus extra for dusting
8 eggs, at room temperature
200g superfine sugar
pinch of salt
230g type 00 flour, plus extra for the pan
20g cocoa powder
35g milk
finely grated zest of ½ organic orange

Preheat the oven to 350°F (170°C). Grease a 10-in (25-cm) fluted tube pan generously with butter and dust with flour.

FOR THE CAKE Cream the butter and powdered sugar in the bowl of a stand mixer for about 5 minutes. Separate the eggs. Gradually stir the yolks into the butter and sugar mixture. Whisk the egg whites with the superfine sugar and salt in a scrupulously clean bowl until holding soft peaks. Sift the flour twice into a bowl, then fold it into the butter and egg yolk mixture. Carefully fold in the egg whites.

Weigh half of the mixture (about 500g) into a separate bowl. Stir the cocoa and milk together in a small bowl until smooth, then fold this mixture along with the orange zest into one half of the cake mixture.

Scoop alternating spoonfuls of the two cake mixtures into the pan. Then draw a wooden skewer through the mixture in circular movements to create the typical marbled effect. Bake on the lowest shelf of the oven for 1 hour–1 hour 10 minutes until a skewer inserted into the cake comes out clean. If the cake starts to brown too much, cover the surface with foil until done.

Let the cake cool in the pan for about 30 minutes, then remove from the pan to cool completely. Dust the bundt cake with powdered sugar to serve.

For a more modern, spicy note, add the finely ground seeds of 4 cardamom pods.

Chocolate Cherry Cake

When summer comes to Vienna and ripe cherries hang from the trees, it's the ideal moment to immerse these juicy fruits in a luscious chocolate cake. This is a very simple cake that adds a sweet touch to any summer picnic.

For 1 cake

FOR THE CAKE

50g dark chocolate (at least 65 percent cocoa)
4 eggs, at room temperature
200g butter, at room temperature, plus extra for greasing
180g superfine sugar
seeds from ½ vanilla bean
120g sour cream
1 tsp finely grated organic lemon zest
pinch of salt
280g type 00 flour
20g cocoa powder
2 tsp baking powder
500g sweet cherries
handful of sliced almonds
powdered sugar for dusting (optional)

Preheat the oven to 350°F (175°C). Grease a 10-in (25-cm) square baking pan generously with butter and line with parchment paper.

FOR THE CAKE Roughly chop the chocolate, then melt in a metal bowl set over a pan of hot water. Let cool slightly.

Separate the eggs. Cream the butter, sugar, and vanilla in the bowl of a stand mixer for 5–7 minutes until light and fluffy. Gradually add the egg yolks and continue beating for another 3 minutes until the mixture is pale, thick, and creamy. Now add the sour cream and lemon zest, stirring only until everything is well combined.

Whisk the egg whites with the salt in a scrupulously clean bowl until stiff.

Sift the flour, cocoa powder, and baking powder into a bowl, then stir into the egg yolk mixture. Fold in half the egg whites to lighten the mixture. Fold in the melted chocolate, then carefully fold in the remaining egg whites.

Pour the cake batter into the prepared pan, spread evenly, and dot with the cherries. Finally, sprinkle with sliced almonds. Bake on the middle shelf of the oven for about 45 minutes until a skewer inserted into the cake comes out clean. Let the cake cool in the pan for 10 minutes, then remove from the pan to cool completely. Dust with powdered sugar to serve if desired.

This recipe is also suitable as a sheet cake. The end result will be a little flatter, and the cooking time should be reduced slightly.

Baked Quark Cheesecake

In this traditional Austrian cheesecake, a sweet and creamy quark filling is encased in a crisp and delicate shortcrust pastry for the ultimate in indulgence. Lemon and vanilla are a fresh and harmonious flavor combination. This cheesecake is best enjoyed lukewarm.

For 1 cheesecake

FOR THE SHORTCRUST PASTRY

100g cold butter, plus room-temperature butter for greasing

1 egg

180g type 00 flour, plus extra for the work surface

pinch of salt

50g powdered sugar, plus extra for dusting (optional)

FOR THE FILLING

2 eggs

50g superfine sugar

80g powdered sugar

250g full-fat quark (20 percent) or other curd cheese

250g sour cream

seeds from ½ vanilla bean

finely grated zest of ½ organic lemon

10g cornstarch

Line the bottom of a deep 8-in (20-cm) springform pan with parchment paper, and grease the sides with butter.

FOR THE PASTRY Cut the butter into cubes. Separate the egg. Mix the flour with the salt and rub into the butter using your fingertips. Now mix in the powdered sugar, add the egg yolk, and work everything together quickly to make a smooth dough.

Roll out the pastry on a floured work surface until it is about ⅛ in (4 mm) thick. Cut a circle of pastry the same size as your pan and place it in the base of the pan. Cut strips from the remaining pastry and use these to line the sides of the pan. Press the sides and the base of the pastry firmly together. Prick the base several times with a fork. Whisk the egg white and brush over the base. Transfer the pastry-lined pan to the fridge and chill for about 30 minutes.

Preheat the oven to 350°F (170°C).

FOR THE FILLING Separate the eggs. Whisk the egg whites and superfine sugar in a scrupulously clean bowl until stiff. In a second bowl, beat the egg yolks and powdered sugar until light and creamy. Now add the quark, sour cream, vanilla, and lemon zest and stir briefly. Fold the egg whites and cornstarch into the quark mixture. Spread the filling over the pastry base.

Bake the cheesecake on the middle shelf of the oven for 50 minutes–1 hour until the filling wobbles slightly like a custard and the pastry around the edge is golden brown.

Remove from the oven and let cool in the pan. Dust with powdered sugar to serve, or just enjoy the cheesecake as it is.

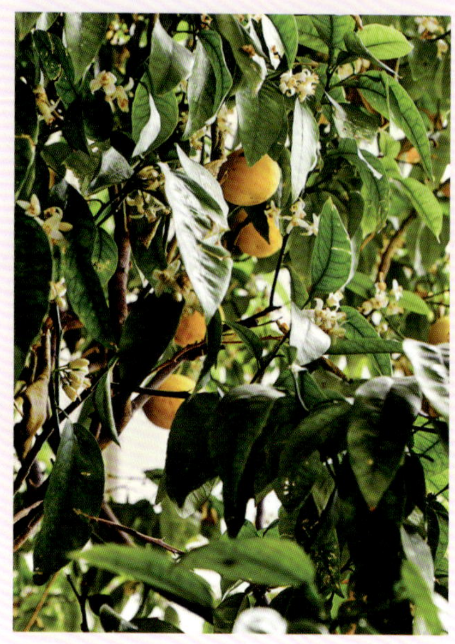

Lemons are an important part of Viennese culture and lifestyle. They were widely used in the past, and that continues to be true today. At a Viennese coffee house, it is just as commonplace to order a soda lemon (soda water with freshly squeezed lemon juice) as it is to request what the locals call a *Kleiner Brauner* (espresso with a splash of milk).

Citrus plants have been cultivated at the Schönbrunn Palace since the 16th century. The orangery still houses an impressive collection of all kinds of citrus trees.

Lemon Cake

This lemon cake is suitable at any time of year. Whether it's for a sweet breakfast or for afternoon tea or a picnic—this quick cake stays particularly moist thanks to the almonds, oil, and sour cream incorporated in the mix. If you like, this cake can also be decorated with candied lemon peel.

For 1 cake

FOR THE CAKE

160g superfine sugar
1 organic lemon
3 eggs, at room temperature
150g type 00 flour
1 tsp baking powder
½ tsp baking soda
65g ground blanched almonds
85g neutral oil, plus extra for greasing
200g sour cream

Preheat the oven to 350°F (170°C). Brush a 4 x 9-in (10 x 22-cm) loaf pan with oil and line with parchment paper.

FOR THE CAKE Add the superfine sugar to the bowl of a stand mixer. Grate the lemon zest directly into the bowl and massage it into the sugar by hand for a few seconds. Now add the eggs and beat the mixture for 5–7 minutes until light and fluffy.

Sift the flour, baking powder, and baking soda into a bowl, then mix in the ground almonds. Add the oil, sour cream, and freshly squeezed juice of the lemon to the beaten egg mixture and stir briefly. Fold in the flour mixture. Transfer the cake batter to the loaf pan and bake on the middle shelf of the oven for 50 minutes, or until a skewer inserted into the cake comes out clean.

Let the cake cool down in the pan for about 10 minutes, then lift it out using the parchment paper and leave on a wire rack to cool completely.

Instead of almonds, pistachios also work wonderfully in this cake. A little crushed cardamom transforms this classic recipe into something very sophisticated. The lemon can be replaced by organic orange, lime, or grapefruit.

For a modern variation, use olive oil and replace the sour cream with Greek yogurt or ricotta.

Rehrücken

The name of this cake means "saddle of venison." Once covered in chocolate ganache and spiked with sliced almonds, it is easy to see why! This delicious and elegant cake goes well with a morning coffee or as a dessert for a festive occasion. Almost every Viennese granny has her own recipe, which is passed down from generation to generation.

For 1 cake

FOR THE CAKE

100g dark chocolate
4 eggs, at room temperature
100g superfine sugar, divided
120g butter, at room temperature, plus extra for greasing
2 tsp vanilla sugar (see p.200)
pinch of ground cinnamon
pinch of salt
25g type 00 flour, plus extra for the pan
15g cornstarch
150g ground almonds

TO ASSEMBLE

100g strained apricot jam (see pp.207–209)
200g dark chocolate
30g coconut oil
50g sliced almonds

Preheat the oven to 350°F (170°C). Brush a Rehrücken pan or a 12-in (30-cm) loaf pan with oil and dust with flour.

FOR THE CAKE Roughly chop the chocolate, then melt in a metal bowl set over a pan of hot water. Let cool slightly.

Separate the eggs. Whisk the egg whites and 50g of the superfine sugar in a scrupulously clean bowl until holding soft peaks. In a second bowl, cream the butter, remaining superfine sugar, vanilla sugar, cinnamon, and salt until light and fluffy. Slowly add the melted chocolate. Gradually stir in the egg yolks, then fold in the whisked egg whites.

Sift the flour and cornstarch into a bowl, then mix in the ground almonds. Fold the dry ingredients into the wet mixture. Transfer into the pan and bake on the middle shelf of the oven for about 50 minutes until a skewer inserted into the cake comes out clean.

Let the cake cool in the pan for about 15 minutes until lukewarm, then turn it out onto a wire rack with a sheet of parchment paper underneath (this is a good way to catch and reuse any glaze that might drip).

TO ASSEMBLE Warm the apricot jam in a small pan and spread thinly over the lukewarm cake. Let the cake cool completely for about 1 hour.

Roughly chop the chocolate and melt this with the coconut oil in a pan over the lowest heat. Quickly cover the cooled cake with an even layer of the icing, and decorate with the sliced almonds. Let set at room temperature.

How to make ...

Basic cake batter

This basic cake batter is incredibly versatile and serves as the basis for all kinds of popular classic cakes. Some cake batters are made with butter or oil, others use whipping cream, sour cream, or yogurt. The one thing they all have in common is their simplicity and moist texture.

The essentials

Room temperature

All ingredients should be at room temperature to prevent the mixture from curdling. The resulting cake will be lighter and have a better texture. It will cook more evenly and the flavor will be better too.

If the butter is cold and firm, it will not combine properly with the sugar or develop its full flavor. The cake batter itself will not be as light and airy.

If the eggs are too cold, they will not mix well with the other ingredients. This can make the mixture lumpy rather than nice and creamy.

Baking powder and baking soda also react better with warm ingredients, so the cake will rise better later. For this reason, it is best to remove butter and eggs from the fridge at least 30 minutes before baking.

Mixing time

To avoid the cake becoming too dense, you should avoid mixing the ingredients for too long at the end. However, fat, sugar, and eggs should be whisked thoroughly until they are light and creamy; this can easily take 10 minutes. Once the flour has been added, do not stir the mixture for long and use a low setting if using an electric mixer. Bake as soon as possible to achieve the best texture.

Sifting flour

Sifting removes any lumps in the flour that could otherwise spoil the mixture. It also ensures the ingredients can bond better, and results in a lighter texture.

Testing with a skewer

Every oven is different, so you should always test your cake with a skewer. This can be done by inserting a wooden skewer or knitting needle into the center of the cake—if it comes out clean, the cake is ready. If it comes out covered in cake batter, the cake needs another 5–10 minutes.

Variations

The basic cake batter can be refined with all sorts of different flavors, such as lemon or orange zest, rum, candied fruits, almonds, or other nuts.

- As long as it is well-wrapped, the cake will keep for a few days and is often even more moist on the second day.
- Basic cake batters are really versatile, they work just as well in a sheet or springform pan as they do in a loaf or fluted tube pan. The only thing that changes is the baking time.

1. Put all the ingredients for the cake into a bowl as indicated in the recipe.

2. Whisk until you have a smooth, silky consistency.

3. Brush a loaf pan with melted butter or oil.

4. Line the pan with parchment paper.

5. Transfer the cake batter into the pan.

6. Test with a skewer toward the end of the baking time to see if the cake is ready.

7. If the skewer comes out clean, the cake is ready. Otherwise, it needs another 5–10 minutes.

8. Remove the slightly cooled cake from the pan with the help of the parchment paper.

9. Remove the parchment paper and let the cake cool.

Raspberry Cake

Raspberries were already being cultivated in the gardens of the Vienna Hofburg back in the 16th century. Over time, numerous recipes were developed for cakes, tarts, desserts, jams, syrups, and ice cream, to name just a few. Here we have a quick cake recipe, where all you need is a bowl to mix the ingredients. The raspberries can also easily be replaced by blueberries, blackberries, gooseberries, cherries, peaches, apricots, or plums.

For 1 cake

FOR THE CAKE

170g butter, at room temperature, plus extra for greasing
pinch of salt
170g superfine sugar
finely grated zest of ½ organic lemon
seeds from 1 vanilla bean
4 eggs, at room temperature
220g type 00 flour
10g baking powder
150g buttermilk
250g raspberries
powdered sugar for dusting (optional)

Preheat the oven to 350°F (180°C). Grease a 12-in (30-cm) loaf pan with butter and line with parchment paper.

FOR THE CAKE Beat the butter, salt, sugar, lemon zest, and vanilla in a stand mixer with the balloon whisk attachment for 5 minutes until light and fluffy. Gradually add the eggs, stirring in well. Sift the flour and baking powder into a bowl, then add to the wet mixture in batches, alternating with the buttermilk. Stir until there are no dry spots visible.

Transfer to the prepared loaf pan and smooth the surface. Sprinkle the raspberries on top and press gently into the batter. Bake on the middle shelf of the oven for 50 minutes–1 hour until golden and a skewer inserted into the cake comes out clean.

Let the cake cool in the pan for about 15 minutes, then lift it out using the parchment paper and transfer to a wire rack to cool completely. Serve dusted with powdered sugar as desired.

Health Cake

I never really understood why this simple cake had been given this name. But then I found out that in the past, the large number of eggs included was considered very healthy. And the eggs make for a beautiful texture, as well as a lovely yellow color. Plenty of lemon also adds a fresh, light touch. So, here's to the good old days.

For 1 cake

FOR THE CAKE

140g butter, at room temperature, plus extra for greasing
150g powdered sugar
6 eggs, at room temperature
350g type 00 flour
10g baking powder
250g milk
100g superfine sugar
finely grated zest of ½ organic lemon
very fine breadcrumbs for the pan

Preheat the oven to 350°F (170°C). Grease an 8½-in (21-cm) fluted tube pan with butter and dust with very fine breadcrumbs.

FOR THE CAKE Beat the butter and powdered sugar in the bowl of a stand mixer for 7–8 minutes until pale and creamy. Separate the eggs. Gradually add the yolks to the butter and sugar mixture, stirring each one in well.

Sift the flour and baking powder in a bowl, then add to the mixture in batches, alternating with the milk. Whisk the egg whites with the superfine sugar in a scrupulously clean bowl until holding soft peaks, then fold into the cake batter along with the lemon zest.

Transfer the mixture to the prepared pan and bake on the middle shelf of the oven for 1 hour–1 hour 10 minutes until a skewer inserted into the cake comes out clean. Let the cake cool in the pan for about 15 minutes, then remove it from the pan to cool for about 1 hour.

Bishop's Bread

This sweet, aromatic sponge cake is not actually a bread at all. It was originally baked in monasteries on St. Martin's Day and at Christmas and Easter. It would be handed out to people as a gesture of sharing and togetherness—a custom that is well worth upholding, including at other times of the year. After all, a homemade offering never fails to please.

For 1 loaf

FOR THE SPONGE

50g raisins
1 tsp rum
4 eggs, at room temperature
40g powdered sugar, plus extra for dusting
seeds from ½ vanilla bean
finely grated zest of ½ organic lemon
40g superfine sugar
1 tsp aniseed
30g butter, plus room-temperature butter for greasing
50g dark chocolate (at least 65 percent cocoa)
100g candied lemons and/or oranges
50g sliced almonds
110g type 00 flour

FOR THE SPONGE Soak the raisins in rum for about 20 minutes.

Preheat the oven to 350°F (170°C). Grease a 12-in (30-cm) loaf pan with butter and line with parchment paper.

Separate the eggs. Cream the egg yolks in a bowl with the powdered sugar, vanilla, and lemon zest until light and fluffy. Whisk the egg whites and superfine sugar in a scrupulously clean bowl until holding soft (not stiff) peaks.

Slightly crush the aniseed using a pestle and mortar, but do not grind too finely. Melt the butter over low heat. Roughly chop the chocolate and candied citrus fruits, then fold these into the egg yolk mixture along with the rum-infused raisins, aniseed, and sliced almonds. Gently fold the egg whites and flour into the mixture in alternating batches. Fold in the melted butter.

Transfer the mixture to the loaf pan and bake on the middle shelf of the oven for 35–40 minutes. Let cool in the pan for about 15 minutes, then remove while still warm and serve dusted with powdered sugar.

Austrian Plum Cake

The classic Austrian cake features soft dough flecked with sweet, ripe plums. Very often, but not always, it is topped with a cinnamon-spiced crumble. And of course, this recipe also works beautifully with apricots, cherries, or plums.

FOR THE DOUGH Melt the butter over low heat. Add the milk. Put the remaining ingredients in the bowl of a stand mixer and add the butter and milk mixture. Knead the dough for 3 minutes on a low setting (using the dough hook attachment). Cover the dough with plastic wrap, let rest for 5 minutes, then knead for another 7 minutes until ready. Shape the dough into a ball, cover, and let rise in a warm place for about 40 minutes.

Knead the dough once more on a floured work surface, cover, and let rise for about 30 minutes.

FOR THE CRUMBLE Meanwhile, slice the butter into cubes and use your fingertips to rub it into the other ingredients. Refrigerate until ready to use.

Line a 13 × 18 in (30 × 40 cm) baking sheet with parchment paper.

FOR THE TOPPING Slice the plums in half and remove the stones.

Roll out the dough on a floured work surface until it is about ⅜ in (8 mm) thick and fits the size of the baking sheet, then place it on the lined baking sheet. Place the plums tightly together on the dough, cut-side up. Press them down slightly, then sprinkle over the crumble. Let prove for about 20 minutes.

Preheat the oven to 350°F (180°C).

Bake on the middle shelf of the oven for 30–40 minutes until golden brown. Dust with powdered sugar while still warm.

If any crumble is left over, this can easily be frozen for future use.

For 1 sheet cake

FOR THE YEAST DOUGH

50g butter
110g milk
10g fresh yeast (see p.110 for converting to dried)
50g superfine sugar
300g all-purpose flour, plus extra for the work surface
pinch of salt
2 tsp finely grated organic lemon zest
1 egg
1 egg yolk

FOR THE CRUMBLE

80g cold butter
100g all-purpose flour
50g superfine sugar
pinch of salt
½ tsp ground cinnamon

FOR THE TOPPING

1kg plums
powdered sugar for dusting

Apple Pie

This dish has a long tradition in Vienna and was already popular in the city's coffee houses in the 18th century. Since then, the ease with which this recipe can be created (as well as its delicious flavor) have made it a favorite in urban and rural communities.

For 1 apple pie

FOR THE SHORTCRUST PASTRY

180g cold butter, plus room-temperature butter for greasing

2 eggs

350g type 00 flour, plus extra for the work surface

pinch of salt

120g powdered sugar, plus extra for dusting

FOR THE FILLING

1kg acidic apples (e.g. Granny Smith, Braeburn, or Jonathan)

1 organic lemon

50g light brown sugar

½ tsp ground cinnamon

Line the bottom of a deep 8-in (20-cm) springform pan with parchment paper, and grease the sides with butter.

FOR THE PASTRY Cut the butter into cubes. Separate one egg. Mix the flour with salt and rub into the butter between your fingertips. Now mix in the powdered sugar, add the egg yolk and the whole egg, and work everything together quickly to make a smooth dough.

Roll out the pastry on a floured work surface until it is about ⅛ in (4 mm) thick. Cut a circle of pastry the same size as your pan and place it inside the base of the pan. Cut enough strips from the rolled-out pastry to line the edge of the pan. Press the sides and base of the pastry firmly together. Combine the remaining pastry scraps in a ball and wrap in plastic wrap. Prick the bottom several times with a fork and chill along with the rest of the pastry for about 30 minutes.

Preheat the oven to 350°F (180°C).

FOR THE FILLING Peel the apples and thinly slice them directly into a large bowl, working around the core. Finely grate 1 teaspoon of lemon zest over the apples and drizzle with freshly squeezed lemon juice. Add the sugar and cinnamon and toss to combine.

Take the pastry out of the fridge, whisk the remaining egg white and use this to brush the base of the tart. Arrange the sliced apples evenly on the pastry base. Roll out the remaining pastry on a floured work surface until it is about ⅛–¼ in (4–5 mm) thick. Cut out a circle the size of the springform pan. Brush the top edge of the pastry in the pan with egg white. Carefully place the circle of pastry on the tart, pressing the edges together to create a wave shape. Prick the pastry several times with a fork to allow air to escape during baking. Bake on the middle shelf of the oven for about 1 hour until golden brown.

Let cool in the pan for at least 1 hour. Dust with powdered sugar to serve.

Strawberry Tartlets

During peak strawberry season, the fruit is best eaten right away while fresh and ripe. You should also make as much jam as possible to see you through the rest of the year. These little tarts combine both options: crisp shortcrust pastry is spread with strawberry jam, topped with fresh strawberries, and served with whipped cream.

For 6 tartlets

FOR THE SHORTCRUST PASTRY

125g cold butter
250g type 00 flour, plus extra for the work surface
50g powdered sugar
pinch of salt
1 small egg
dried beans for blind baking

FOR THE TOPPING

500g strawberries
120g strawberry jam
200g whipping cream
2 tsp vanilla sugar *(see p.200)*

FOR THE PASTRY Cut the butter into cubes and use your fingertips to rub it into the flour, powdered sugar, and salt. Add the egg, and work everything together swiftly until you have a smooth dough. If the pastry is too dry, add 1–2 tablespoons of cold water. Wrap the pastry in plastic wrap and refrigerate for about 1 hour.

Preheat the oven to 350°F (170°C).

Roll out the dough on a floured work surface until it is ⅛ in (3–4 mm) thick, then cut out 5-in (12-cm) circles. Combine the leftover pastry and repeat this process until you have six pastry circles. Line six 3¼-in (8-cm) tartlet pans with the pastry, cover with parchment paper, and fill with dried beans. Bake on the middle shelf of the oven for 10–15 minutes until the edges are browning slightly. Remove the parchment paper and beans and continue baking for another 5–10 minutes, then cool completely before carefully lifting the pastry cases out of the pans.

FOR THE TOPPING Prepare the strawberries by slicing them into quarters or halves, or leaving them whole, depending on the size. Spread about 1 tablespoon of strawberry jam on each of the tartlets. Arrange the strawberries decoratively on the jam.

Whisk the whipping cream with the vanilla sugar until creamy but not too firm, and serve alongside the tartlets.

Smooth out some paper baking cups and use these instead of parchment paper to line the pastry.

Drunken Capuchin Cakes

Monks with their traditional hooded cloaks have been a source of inspiration for various recipe names in Austria: you can order a Kapuziner *(double mocha with whipped cream topping), a* Kapuzinerstrudel *(traditional sweet Austrian pastry), or a* Besoffene Kapuziner *(drunken Capuchin), which is the dish we describe here. This particular recipe is also known as the "Thirsty Nun," "Drunken Hansl," or "Drunken Liesl" and features little cakes soaked in a spicy liquid of wine, cider, or apple juice.*

For 6 little cakes

FOR THE CAKE

30g butter, at room temperature
½ vanilla bean
2 eggs, at room temperature
20g powdered sugar
pinch of salt
pinch of ground cinnamon
1 tsp finely grated organic lemon zest
70g type 00 flour
40g finely ground walnuts
60g fine breadcrumbs
75g milk

FOR THE SPICED WINE

500g Grüner Veltliner
70g powdered sugar
1 strip of organic lemon zest
1 cinnamon stick
1 clove
1 star anise

TO SERVE

150g whipping cream
1 tsp superfine sugar

Preheat the oven to 350°F (175°C). Prepare an ice-water bath.

FOR THE CAKE Melt the butter over moderate heat. Lightly brush six mini fluted tube pans, about 2¼-in (6-cm) diameter, with melted butter. Set the remaining melted butter aside to cool.

Slice the vanilla bean in half lengthwise and scrape out the seeds with a small, sharp knife. Set the empty pod aside. In a metal bowl set over a pan of hot water, beat the eggs, powdered sugar, vanilla, salt, cinnamon, and lemon zest with a balloon whisk until creamy. Then transfer the bowl to the ice-water bath and continue stirring until cold.

Fold in the flour, walnuts, and breadcrumbs. Finally, fold in the cooled melted butter and the milk. Fill the fluted tube pans so that the mix comes to ½ in (1 cm) below the edge. Bake on the middle shelf of the oven for 20–25 minutes until a skewer inserted in the cakes comes out clean.

FOR THE SPICED WINE Meanwhile, heat the wine in a saucepan with the powdered sugar, lemon zest, cinnamon stick, scraped out vanilla bean, clove, and star anise, and allow the flavors to infuse for about 20 minutes on a very low heat.

Remove the mini bundt cakes from the oven and allow to cool in the pans for about 10 minutes before turning them out of the pans. Transfer into deep bowls and pour over plenty of spiced wine. Let infuse slightly if desired.

TO SERVE Whip the cream with the sugar until creamy, then use this to decorate the cakes.

These little cakes also taste great with cider, and apple juice is another good option if the Capuchin has to drive somewhere after eating dessert. In this case, the sugar can be omitted from the liquid.

Apricot Cream Tart

With its stunning meringue topping, this tart is guaranteed to grab attention. Depending on your preference and the time of year, you can substitute whatever fruit is in season. The crumbs in the base of the tart help prevent the pastry from becoming soggy from the fruit, but they also add a new flavor element of their own.

For 1 tart

FOR THE PASTRY

100g cold butter

200g type 00 flour, plus extra for the work surface

1 tbsp powdered sugar

pinch of salt

2 egg yolks

splash of milk

FOR THE TOPPING

8 apricots

3 tbsp cookie crumbs (e.g. graham crackers)

1 tbsp raw cane sugar or Demerara sugar

FOR THE MERINGUE

60g egg whites (from about 2 eggs)

pinch of salt

45g powdered sugar, plus extra for dusting

45g superfine sugar

FOR THE PASTRY Cube the butter and use your fingertips to rub it into the flour, powdered sugar, and salt. Add the egg yolks and work everything together until smoothly combined, adding some milk if necessary. Roll out the pastry on a lightly floured work surface until it is 1⁄16–1⁄8 in (2–3 mm) thick. Line a 9-in (23-cm) tart pan with the pastry and refrigerate for 20 minutes.

Preheat the oven to 350°F (180°C).

FOR THE TOPPING Cut the apricots in half, remove the stones, and slice into wedges. Prick the pastry base several times with a fork. Sprinkle with the cookie crumbs. Arrange the apricots on top and sprinkle with the cane sugar. Bake on the middle shelf for 20–25 minutes until the edge is browning slightly. Remove from the oven and increase the temperature to 400°F (200°C) using the top heating element or broiler setting.

FOR THE MERINGUE Use an electric hand mixer to beat the egg whites, salt, and both sugars in a scrupulously clean metal bowl set over a pan of hot water until the sugar has dissolved completely. Continue whisking the mixture in a stand mixer (using the balloon whisk attachment) for 10–15 minutes until it reaches meringue consistency.

Spread the meringue mixture over the tart in a decorative wave pattern. Cook on the top shelf of the oven for 3–5 minutes until the tips of the meringue start to brown. Let cool slightly, then remove from the pan and dust with powdered sugar.

If you are looking for a faster, easier, but nonetheless excellent option, the meringue can be omitted and the tart served just as it is or with a spoonful of whipped cream. In this case, you can safely use a whole egg instead of the yolks for the shortcrust pastry.

Bienenstich

Running barefoot through summer meadows then tucking into a large slab of Bienenstich cake—that's what comes to mind when I think of my childhood summers. Perhaps the same was true of children in the summer of 1719, when legend has it that a pastry chef set out to make a particularly delicious dessert to celebrate the marriage of Elector Friedrich August III to Maria Josepha of Austria. The Bienenstich (bee sting) cake gets its name because it evokes the colors of the Saxon coat of arms (yellow and black). And it was so popular it spread rapidly throughout Germany and Austria.

FOR THE YEAST DOUGH Melt the butter, then add the milk and set aside. Put the remaining ingredients in the bowl of a stand mixer then add the butter and milk mixture. Knead this mixture on a low setting for 3 minutes (using the dough hook attachment). Let it rest for 5 minutes, then knead again on a medium setting for 7 minutes. Shape the dough into a ball, cover with plastic wrap, and let rise in a warm place for about 1 hour.

Knead the dough once more on a floured work surface, shape it into a ball, cover, and let rise for another 30 minutes.

FOR THE HONEY ALMONDS Heat the butter, honey, and whipping cream in a pan over moderate heat until everything has melted. Add the almonds and simmer over low heat, stirring until the almonds have caramelized slightly. Remove from the heat and let the almond mixture cool down a bit.

Line the bottom of a 10-in (26-cm) springform pan with parchment paper and brush the sides with butter. Knead the yeast dough one final time, then roll it out on a floured work surface until it is about the size of the springform pan. Transfer the dough into the pan, spread the almond mixture evenly on top, cover, and let rise for about 20 minutes.

Preheat the oven to 350°F (180°C).

Bake the cake on the middle shelf of the oven for 25–30 minutes until golden brown. If the almond mixture is browning too much, cover with foil. Remove the cake from the oven and let cool for about 20 minutes in the pan, before releasing from the springform pan and gently transferring the cake, along with the parchment paper, to a wire rack to cool completely.

→

For 1 cake

FOR THE YEAST DOUGH

50g butter, plus extra for greasing
110g milk
15g fresh yeast (see p.110 for converting to dried)
50g superfine sugar
300g all-purpose flour, plus extra for the work surface
pinch of salt
2 tsp finely grated organic lemon zest
1 egg
1 egg yolk

FOR THE HONEY ALMONDS

125g butter
125g honey
2 tbsp whipping cream
200g sliced almonds

FOR THE VANILLA CREAM

400g milk, divided
3 egg yolks
40g cornstarch
1 vanilla bean
80g superfine sugar, divided
250g whipping cream

FOR THE CREAM FILLING Combine 3 tablespoons of milk with the egg yolks and cornstarch in a small bowl, and stir until smooth. Slice the vanilla bean in half lengthwise and scrape out the seeds with a small, sharp knife. Put the vanilla bean and seeds in a saucepan with the remaining milk and 60g of the superfine sugar and bring to a simmer. As soon as the milk begins to boil, add 3 tablespoons of the hot milk to the cornstarch and egg yolks to bring this up to temperature. Then put everything in the saucepan and continue cooking, stirring with a balloon whisk, until the mixture begins to thicken to a custard consistency. Transfer the mixture to a bowl, cover the surface with plastic wrap, and let cool (the plastic should be in contact with the surface of the custard to prevent a skin from forming).

Pass the cooled mixture through a fine mesh strainer or process with an immersion blender. Beat the whipping cream with the remaining sugar until stiff, then fold into the cooled custard.

Slice the cake in half horizontally. Transfer the base to a cake plate. Place a cake ring around the cake and line with parchment paper. Spread the creamy custard mixture over the cake then add the top cake layer. Now tighten the cake ring slightly to make sure the creamy filling and the two cake layers are neatly sealed. Cover and refrigerate the cake for at least 1 hour.

Carefully release the cake ring and peel off the parchment paper to serve.

SCHICHT

Linzer Torte

The recipe for Linzer Torte is considered to be one of the oldest known baking recipes in the world. Its origins are said to go back to a cookbook by Countess Ann Margarita Sagramosa from 1653, and that's why this tart is so steeped in history. But one thing that never changes is the combination of exquisite spices in the dough and the classic red currant jam.

For 1 tart

FOR THE SHORTCRUST PASTRY

150g almonds or hazelnuts
150g cold butter
300g type 00 flour, plus extra for working
120g powdered sugar
1 generous tsp ground cinnamon
pinch of ground cloves
pinch of salt
1 tsp finely grated organic orange zest
3g baking powder
1 egg

FOR THE FILLING AND FOR SPRINKLING

250g red currant jam (see p.208)
1 egg white
60g sliced almonds

If you do not have a food processor, you can also use ground hazelnuts or almonds.

Preheat the oven to 350°F (180°C). Line a baking sheet with parchment paper.

FOR THE PASTRY Spread the almonds or hazelnuts on the lined baking sheet and roast on the middle shelf of the oven for 8–10 minutes. Remove from the oven and let cool completely, then grind to a fine consistency in a food processor.

Cut the butter into cubes and use your fingertips to rub this into the flour, ground nuts, powdered sugar, spices, salt, orange zest, and baking powder. Add the egg and work everything swiftly together until you have a smooth dough. If the pastry is too dry, add 1–2 tablespoons of cold water. Wrap the pastry in plastic wrap and refrigerate for about 1 hour.

Preheat the oven again to 350°F (180°C). Line the bottom of a 9½-in (24-cm) springform pan with parchment paper.

Roll out the pastry on a floured work surface until it is ¼ in (5–6 mm) thick. When rolling the pastry, keep lifting it slightly to avoid it sticking to the work surface. Cut a circle of pastry the same size as your pan and place it inside the lined pan with the help of the rolling pin. Press the pastry flat over the base of the pan.

FOR THE FILLING Spread the jam over the pastry base. Combine the leftover pastry pieces, shape into long strands, and arrange these in a grid pattern on top of the jam. Trim any excess ends of pastry. Create another long strand of pastry from the leftovers and position it around the edge of the tart, pressing down slightly. Then brush with the egg white. Sprinkle with the sliced almonds and bake on the middle shelf of the oven for 45–50 minutes. Let cool in the pan for about 1 hour.

Tortes

A typical Sunday activity in Vienna might involve a stroll through the *erste Bezirk* (first district) as the city center is known. Usual features on an outing of this kind include a Viennese coffee and a lavish slice of Imperial Torte (see p.73), Dobos Torte (see p.56), or Sachertorte (see p.64) with cream, often enjoyed at a round marble table in a cozy niche at one of the many coffee houses.

Dobos Torte

The Dobos Torte, invented in 1884 by Hungarian pastry chef József C. Dobos, is a classic example of the bakery of the Austro-Hungarian monarchy: a dessert consisting of seven thin sponge layers, filled with chocolate butter cream and topped with crisp caramel. This delicious and elegant cake is still perfect for special occasions today.

For 1 cake

FOR THE SPONGE

7 large eggs
225g superfine sugar, divided
seeds from ½ vanilla bean
160g type 00 flour
generous pinch of salt
75g butter

FOR THE CARAMEL

100g superfine sugar
30g water
neutral oil for working with the caramel

FOR THE CHOCOLATE CREAM

90g egg whites, at room temperature (from about 3 eggs)
pinch of salt
140g superfine sugar
150g dark chocolate (at least 65 percent cocoa)
270g butter, at room temperature
1 tsp rum

TO DECORATE

50g hazelnuts

Prepare eight sheets of parchment paper. Place a deep 8-in (20-cm) cake ring on each sheet in turn and draw a circle around it with a pencil. Turn the sheets of parchment paper over so the pencil lines are now underneath. Preheat the oven to 350°F (180°C).

FOR THE SPONGE Separate the eggs. Whisk the egg yolks, 200g of the superfine sugar, and vanilla in the bowl of a stand mixer for 5 minutes until light and creamy. Sift the flour and add to the yolk mixture along with the salt.

Beat the egg whites with the remaining 25g of sugar in a scrupulously clean bowl until they are holding their shape, then carefully fold into the egg yolk mixture in two stages. Melt the butter in a saucepan over low heat and fold in about 250g of the sponge mixture. Now fold the butter mixture back into the rest of the sponge mixture.

Line a baking sheet with one of the prepared sheets of parchment paper. Transfer about 100g of the mixture into the center of the pencil circle, spreading it as evenly as possible to the edge of the circle using an angled palette knife. Bake on the middle shelf of the oven for 5–7 minutes until the edge is beginning to go brown. Remove the sponge base from the pan (keep it on the parchment paper) and allow the pan to cool slightly. Proceed in the same way with the rest of the sponge mixture and the remaining sheets of parchment paper.

Allow the sponge bases to cool completely, then carefully remove them from the parchment paper using the palette knife.

→

FOR THE CARAMEL Stir the sugar and water in a saucepan over medium heat for about 5 minutes until you have a golden brown caramel. Quickly pour the very hot caramel (be careful when working with it!) into the center of one of the baked sponge layers and spread it out smoothly using an oiled palette knife. Now use an oiled sharp knife to cut it into 12 slices. If the caramel becomes too brittle and can no longer be cut easily, the caramel cake layer can be warmed briefly in the oven for 30 seconds (in the residual heat or set to very low). This should enable you to cut the caramel again without any risk of breakage.

FOR THE CHOCOLATE CREAM Use a hand mixer to beat the egg whites, salt, and sugar in a scrupulously clean bowl over a pan of hot water until the sugar has dissolved completely. Continue whisking the mixture in a stand mixer (using the balloon whisk attachment) for about 20 minutes until it reaches a meringue consistency.

Meanwhile, roughly chop the chocolate, melt it in a metal bowl over a pan of hot water, then let cool slightly.

Now gradually add the very soft butter to the meringue. (After adding about half the butter, the meringue will look like it has collapsed—that's normal. Just keep whisking, add the remaining butter, and let the stand mixer run until the meringue is nice and creamy again.) Add the cooled chocolate and the rum and stir until smooth.

LAYERING Place the first sponge base on a cake plate. Spread 2 tablespoons of the chocolate cream over the surface and place another sponge layer on top. Repeat until all seven sponge layers are stacked and coated. Use an angled palette knife to apply a thin layer of chocolate cream all around the cake then cover with strips of parchment paper. Place the cake ring around the cake and tighten well. Refrigerate for at least 2 hours. (Cover the remaining chocolate cream and set aside at room temperature or in the fridge in very warm weather.)

TO DECORATE Roast the hazelnuts in the oven at 300°F (150°C) for 10 minutes. Then chop roughly.

Release the cake from the cake ring and peel off the parchment paper. Whisk the chocolate cream again and transfer 6 tablespoons into a piping bag fitted with a star nozzle. Use an angled palette knife to cover the cake in a smooth layer of the remaining chocolate cream. Add the chopped nuts to the side of the cake. Use the piping bag to create 12 little swirls on the cake, then arrange the caramel slices on the cake. Finish with a final swirl of chocolate cream in the center of the cake.

Strawberry Cream Cake

This is the perfect cake for festive occasions in early summer and is a guaranteed crowd pleaser.

For 1 cake

FOR THE CAKE

160g milk
80g butter, plus extra for greasing
4 eggs, at room temperature
220g superfine sugar
1 tsp vanilla sugar (see p.200)
220g type 00 flour
8g baking powder
pinch of salt
1 tsp finely grated organic lemon zest

FOR THE FILLING

500g whipping cream
200g powdered sugar, divided
500g mascarpone
1 tsp vanilla sugar (see p.200)
1 tsp finely grated organic orange zest
1 tsp finely grated organic lemon zest
500g strawberries
150g strawberry jam

Preheat the oven to 350°F (170°C). Line the bottom of an 8-in (20-cm) springform pan with parchment paper and brush the sides with butter.

FOR THE CAKE Heat the milk and butter in a small saucepan until the butter has melted but the milk is not yet boiling. Whisk the eggs, superfine sugar, and vanilla sugar in the bowl of a stand mixer for 8 minutes until creamy. Sift the flour and baking powder into a bowl, then carefully fold into the egg and sugar mixture along with the salt and lemon zest.

Put the milk and butter mixture into a bowl and quickly but carefully fold in one-third of the egg, sugar, and flour mixture. Add this mixture back into the remaining egg, sugar, and flour mixture and stir until smooth. Transfer into the prepared pan and bake on the middle shelf of the oven for 35–40 minutes until a skewer inserted into the cake comes out clean.

Let the cake cool in the pan for about 30 minutes, then release from the pan and let cool completely for 1 hour.

FOR THE FILLING Whip the cream with 100g of powdered sugar until thick and creamy but not stiff. Combine the mascarpone with the remaining 100g of powdered sugar, vanilla sugar, and orange and lemon zest. Carefully stir one-third of the whipped cream into the mascarpone mixture, then fold in the remaining whipped cream. Rinse the strawberries, remove the stems, and thinly slice. Cut the cake twice horizontally to create three layers.

Spread half the strawberry jam over the cut surface of the bottom cake layer. Top this with 3–4 tablespoons of the cream mixture, then sprinkle with a few sliced strawberries. Spread 3–4 tablespoons of the cream mixture over one side of the middle cake layer, then place this (cream-side down) on the strawberries. Add another layer of jam, cream, and strawberries, then spread some of the cream mixture over the cut surface of the final cake layer and place this (cream-side down) on top. Use an angled palette knife to cover the cake with the cream mixture. Put the remaining cream mixture in a piping bag fitted with a star nozzle and pipe decoratively onto the cake.

People often remark that "Sachertorte is a piece of Vienna you can take home with you." An understandable sentiment because this cake—with its light chocolate layers filled with apricot jam and covered in a shiny chocolate glaze—is a culinary symbol of Vienna.

Sachertorte

The original Sachertorte recipe is still a secret today. But there are lots of recipes based on the original, including this one.

For 1 cake

FOR THE CAKE

140g dark chocolate
140g butter, at room temperature, plus extra for greasing
40g powdered sugar
7 eggs, at room temperature
160g superfine sugar
pinch of salt
140g type 00 flour
20g cocoa powder

TO ASSEMBLE

200g strained apricot jam (see pp.207–209)
200g superfine sugar
125g water
150g dark chocolate
whipped cream to serve

Preheat the oven to 350°F (170°C). Lightly grease a 9½-in (24-cm) springform pan with butter, and line the bottom and sides with parchment paper.

FOR THE CAKE Roughly chop the chocolate and melt it in a metal bowl over a pan of hot water. Let cool slightly.

Meanwhile, cream the butter and powdered sugar in the bowl of a stand mixer for 8 minutes until light and fluffy. Separate the eggs and stir the yolks into the butter mixture, one after the other. Gradually mix in the melted dark chocolate and stir. You should have a very light and airy mixture.

Whisk the egg whites, superfine sugar, and salt in a scrupulously clean bowl until holding soft (not stiff) peaks. Carefully fold the egg whites into the chocolate mixture in three stages. Sift the flour and cocoa powder into a bowl, then fold these in, too. Transfer the mixture to the prepared pan and bake on the middle shelf of the oven for about 50 minutes until a skewer inserted into the cake comes out clean.

Remove the cake from the oven and let cool for about 20 minutes in the pan. Release from the pan, remove the parchment paper, turn the cake over, and let cool completely on a wire rack. Once cool, slice in half horizontally.

TO ASSEMBLE Heat the apricot jam and stir until smooth. Spread a generous layer of jam over the cut surface of the bottom cake layer. Place the second cake layer on top, cut-surface down. Cover the top and sides of the cake with jam. Refrigerate for at least 1 hour.

Put the superfine sugar and water in a pan and boil vigorously for about 5 minutes. Let cool briefly. Roughly chop the chocolate, gradually add to the warm sugar syrup and stir everything together to make a thick glaze. Pour the entire lukewarm glaze over the cake and quickly spread it over the top and sides with an angled palette knife. Let set for 1–2 hours, then serve with softly whipped cream.

Poppy Seed Cake

This recipe, called Mohntorten *in German, may feel out of place in a chapter of tortes. Nowadays, the German word "torte" (likely derived from the Latin "torta," meaning round loaf or bread product) is mostly associated with elaborate, cream-filled layer cakes. The original "torte," however, was probably a slice of bread, and only became a sweet delicacy after the introduction of inexpensive beet sugar.*

For 1 cake

FOR THE CAKE

6 eggs, at room temperature
pinch of salt
160g superfine sugar, divided
juice of 1 organic lemon and 1 tsp finely grated zest
200g butter, at room temperature, plus extra for greasing
200g ground poppy seeds (available online or grind your own)
100g ground hazelnuts or almonds
100g milk

FOR THE ICING

juice of ½ organic lemon and ½ tsp finely grated zest
100g powdered sugar

Preheat the oven to 350°F (180°C). Line the bottom of a 10-in (26-cm) springform pan with parchment paper and brush the sides with butter.

FOR THE CAKE Separate the eggs. Whisk the egg whites, salt, and 80g of the superfine sugar in a scrupulously clean bowl until stiff.

Cream the lemon zest, butter, and remaining 80g superfine sugar in the bowl of a stand mixer for about 5 minutes until the mixture is pale and creamy. Next, gradually add the egg yolks and combine until smooth. Stir the poppy seeds, nuts, milk, and lemon juice into the mixture. Very carefully fold in the whisked egg whites in two batches.

Transfer the mixture to the pan and bake on the middle shelf of the oven for 30–35 minutes until a skewer inserted into the cake comes out clean. Let the cake cool in the pan for about 1 hour.

FOR THE ICING Combine the lemon juice and powdered sugar and stir until smooth.

Release the springform pan, carefully remove the parchment paper, and place the poppy seed cake on a plate. Spread with lemon icing, leave to set slightly, then sprinkle with the lemon zest.

Spanische Windtorte

In the 19th century, the Spanische Windtorte was described as "the most elegant cake in Vienna"—a creation of meringue and whipped cream which made a wonderful dinner party centerpiece. Although it only contains a few ingredients, it is complex to prepare and requires a certain patience. The cake should be served immediately and is tricky to slice elegantly. This might detract from its appearance, but most certainly not the flavor.

For 1 cake

FOR THE FRENCH MERINGUE

320g egg whites, at room temperature (from about 8 large eggs)

pinch of salt

480g powdered sugar

FOR THE FONDANT VIOLETS

50g white rolled fondant

purple and yellow food coloring

FOR THE SWISS MERINGUE

160g egg whites, at room temperature (from about 4 large eggs)

pinch of salt

250g powdered sugar

FOR THE FILLING

500g whipping cream

50g powdered sugar

1 tsp orange blossom water (optional)

500g strawberries

Prepare three sheets of parchment paper. Use a pencil and an 8-in (20-cm) cake pan or cake ring to draw two circles on each of two of the parchment paper sheets and a single circle on the third sheet—there should be a total of five circles. Turn the sheets of parchment paper over so the pencil lines are now underneath.

Preheat the oven to 275°F (140°C).

FOR THE FRENCH MERINGUE Put the egg whites and salt in the scrupulously clean bowl of a stand mixer, and whisk on the highest setting until the mixture gains volume. Add the powdered sugar and continue mixing until you have a glossy meringue consistency. Put two-thirds of the meringue in a piping bag fitted with a plain round ⅝-in (1.5-cm) nozzle.

Line three baking sheets with the prepared parchment paper. Pipe the meringue in a spiral, working from the outside inward, on the two penciled circles on one baking sheet. (These will later form the bottom and top layers of the cake.)

Pipe the remaining meringue in the bag onto the three other circles, but this time create rings of meringue rather than filling in the circles. (These will later form the sides of the cake when it is stacked.)

Bake the meringues on the top, middle, and bottom oven shelves for about 45 minutes, or until they can be removed easily from the parchment paper. Swap the positions of the baking sheets several times during baking. Remove from the oven and let cool completely.

→

FOR THE VIOLETS Mix 20g of fondant with one drop of purple food color, and another 20g of fondant with two drops of purple food color. Color the remaining 10g of fondant with a single drop of yellow. Shape three small pieces of violet fondant into little balls (approximately the size of a pearl) and press flat with your fingers to form thin disks. Repeat with the purple fondant (these will make the petals of the flower). Now take three small pieces of yellow fondant and shape into balls (these form the center of each flower). Join the petals together to make a circle. Add the yellow balls in the middle to finish each flower. Proceed in the same way with the remaining fondant icing Leave to dry on parchment paper for at least 1 hour.

Meanwhile, carefully place one cooled meringue disk on a 12-in (30-cm) oven-safe, flat serving plate. Put the remaining meringue mixture in a piping bag, and pipe about eight blobs of meringue in a ring around the edge of the disk. Place one of the meringue rings on top and press down slightly. Stack the other two meringue rings on top, sticking each one together with fresh meringue. Pipe the remaining meringue mixture around the outside of the rings and smooth the surface using an angled palette knife. Bake the stacked meringues on the serving plate for about 45 minutes in an oven set to 275°F (140°C). Remove from the oven and allow to cool completely.

FOR THE SWISS MERINGUE Use a hand mixer to beat the egg whites, salt, and powdered sugar in a scrupulously clean bowl over a pan of hot water until the sugar has dissolved completely. Continue whisking the mixture in a stand mixer (using the balloon whisk attachment) for 10–15 minutes until it reaches meringue consistency. Transfer the meringue into a piping bag fitted with a large star nozzle.

Pipe the Swiss meringue mixture decoratively around the baked meringue shell to create three rings at different heights. Place the second meringue disk on a baking sheet lined with parchment paper and pipe a ring of Swiss meringue around the edge, followed by small dollops of meringue on top and in the middle. Bake this disk along with the meringue shell for another 30 minutes in the warm oven. Remove from the oven and let cool completely.

FOR THE FILLING Whisk the whipping cream and powdered sugar in a bowl until soft peaks form. Stir in the orange blossom water if desired. Chop the strawberries into whatever size you prefer, then fold carefully into the cream mixture. Put the strawberries and cream into the cooled meringue shell and place the meringue lid on top.

TO DECORATE Add the violets to the cake with tiny blobs of meringue.

Spanische Windtorte.

Man macht eine Masse von: 10 Eiweiß Schnee schlagen, 1 ℔ Zucker, gut verrühren, in 2 Theile im lauwarmen Ofen backen, etwas davon zum Spritzen überlassen, dann mit 1/2 Seidel Schlagobers, 1/4 ℔ Vanillezucker füllen.

Imperial Torte

The kitchen boys at the luxury Hotel Imperial were absolutely determined to create the perfect cake for Kaiser Franz Joseph I, or so the story goes. A cake that would be so unique, no other confectioner would be able to emulate it. So Xaver Loibner snuck into the kitchen and baked a square cake. The following day, the Kaiser was so enthralled with this creation, it was all he wanted to eat. The original recipe has never been revealed, but I hope Xaver Loibner would be satisfied with my version.

For 1 cake

FOR THE JAPONAISE CAKE

4 egg whites
130g superfine sugar, divided
80g ground blanched almonds

FOR THE CHOCOLATE BUTTERCREAM

250g dark chocolate
250g butter, at room temperature, divided, plus extra for greasing
4 egg yolks
160g water
140g superfine sugar
pinch of salt

TO ASSEMBLE

2 tbsp raspberry jam (see p.208)
1 tbsp marmalade
400g marzipan
200g dark chocolate
20g coconut oil
powdered sugar for the work surface

Preheat the oven to 375°F (190°C). Line a 13 × 18 in (30 × 40 cm) baking sheet with parchment paper.

FOR THE JAPONAISE CAKE Beat the egg whites with 50g of the superfine sugar in a scrupulously clean bowl. Combine the remaining 80g of sugar with the ground almonds and fold into the egg whites. Using an angled palette knife, spread the mixture out smoothly to create a thin ¼-in (5-mm) layer on the lined baking sheet. Bake for 15–20 minutes on the middle shelf until golden, then let cool slightly on the baking sheet. Carefully remove the paper and let the cake cool completely.

FOR THE BUTTERCREAM Roughly chop the chocolate and melt this with 50g of the butter in a metal bowl over a pan of hot water. Let cool slightly.

Beat the egg yolks until pale and creamy. Put the water and sugar in a saucepan and heat to 230°F (110°C) on a sugar thermometer. Do not stir. Pour the hot sugar syrup into the yolks in a thin stream, whisking as you do so. Once all the sugar syrup has been added, continue whisking the mixture until it has cooled down again. Then gradually add the remaining 200g of butter by the spoonful, stirring each time until the mixture is smooth. Finally, add the cooled melted chocolate and the salt, and beat the buttercream for another 5 minutes.

→

Grease a 6-in (15-cm) square cake pan with butter and line it with parchment paper (this makes it easier to turn the cake out of the pan later). Use a serrated knife to cut the almond base into four 6-in (15-cm) squares.

TO ASSEMBLE Put one of the cake bases into the pan and spread with 1 tablespoon of raspberry jam. Next, add about 3 tablespoons of the buttercream on top of the jam and spread it smoothly with an angled palette knife. Place a second cake layer on top of the buttercream. Spread this one with 1 tablespoon of marmalade, and once again top with 3 tablespoons of buttercream. Place another cake layer on top, and spread with 1 tablespoon of raspberry jam and 3 tablespoons of buttercream, then add the final cake layer. Spread with the remaining buttercream, cover with parchment paper or plastic wrap, and chill in the fridge for at least 4 hours or overnight.

Now turn the cake out of the pan. Roll out the marzipan on a work surface that has been dusted with powdered sugar until it is ⅛ in (3–4 mm) thick. Use a rolling pin to lift the marzipan onto the cake, then gently press it into position so it covers the cake in a smooth layer. If necessary, trim any excess marzipan at the edges. Press the sides smooth using a cake scraper. Place the cake on a sheet of parchment paper (so any glaze that drips off can be easily removed and reused later).

Roughly chop the chocolate and melt this with the coconut oil in a pan over the lowest heat. Quickly pour the melted chocolate mixture over the cake, making sure that every section is covered. Let the glaze dry. Slice the cake into cubes to serve.

Any leftover Japonaise cake can be used as a component in Diplomat Pudding (see p.196) or finely crumbled as a base for Apricot Cream Tart (see p.46).

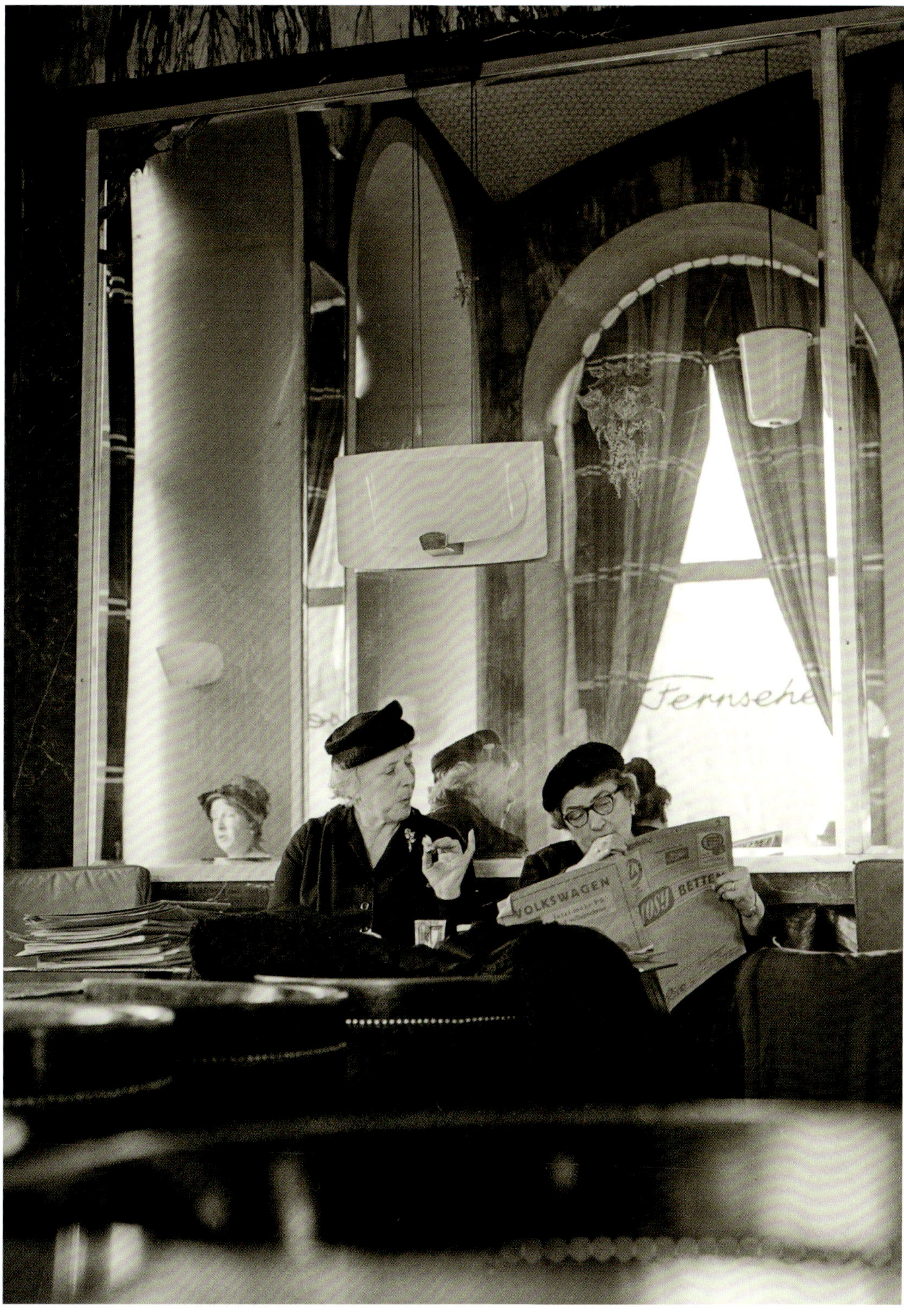
Fernsehe
VOLKSWAGEN
BETTEN

Filling and icing tortes

Step-by-step instructions

The essentials

To fill a torte, the base must first be split horizontally. You will need to decide how many layers the torte should have. Each layer should be at least ¾–1¼ in (2–3 cm) thick. A ratio of ¾-in (2-cm) cake layers to ⅝ in (1.5 cm) of filling is ideal for buttercream tortes. For tortes with whipped cream, the layers and filling are thicker.

Cutting the torte works particularly well using a cake ring with marked recesses. This makes it easy to determine the cutting height and achieve a straight cut. Toothpicks can also be used as a guide. To do this, insert toothpicks horizontally into the torte at regular intervals at the desired height, then slice through the torte at the point above the toothpick markers. Alternatively, run a thread on the toothpicks around the cake, cross the ends, and then pull them apart so the thread cuts through the cake.

How it's done

- Place the base of the cake on a revolving cake plate and spread with jam and/or cream or icing using an angled palette knife, turning the cake plate from time to time to achieve an even layer.
- Use the palette knife to remove any excess icing from the edge and smooth the sides.
- Place the second cake layer precisely on top, press lightly into position and once again apply icing with the palette knife.
- Place additional cake layers as described, filling and covering each in turn. Finally, add the top cake layer and press lightly into position. Add the rest of the icing with the palette knife and make sure it is smooth all around.
- Place a strip of parchment paper around the torte, followed by a cake ring which should be tightened into position. This keeps the cake in shape while it chills and creates straight edges.
- Finally, carefully remove the cake ring and parchment paper and decorate the torte.

- Brush the cake layers with vanilla syrup before filling. This prevents the cake from drying out and gives it a particularly delicious flavor.
- The cake layers can easily be pre-baked and frozen for up to 1 month wrapped in plastic wrap. When ready to use, let the cakes defrost overnight at room temperature.

1. Place a cake cutting ring around the cake.

2. Cut the cake in two to three places, turning the cake ring as you slice through the cake.

3. Spread the base of the cake with jam.

4. Then spread with icing.

5. Place the next cake layer on top.

6. Proceed in the same way with subsequent layers.

7. Spread a layer of icing all around the torte.

8. Place parchment paper around the torte.

9. Tighten the cake ring and refrigerate the torte. This gives it an upright shape and it can be decorated later.

Cream Slices & Roulades

Layer by layer, these baking masterpieces are often accompanied by opulent creams and fillings. One exception to this is the Swiss Roll (see p.94), a classic cake filled with the best quality apricot jam, which stands out precisely for its simplicity, but can still hold its own against its illustrious peers.

Cream Slice

The filled pastry that we refer to nowadays as a cream slice is noted in Therese's little baking book as "Miss Wanda's Cream Slice." The true identity of the mysterious Miss Wanda will probably never be known. Perhaps she attracted people's attention in a similar way to this dessert, with its buttery layers of crisp pastry and exquisite diplomat cream.

For 4 pastries

FOR THE DIPLOMAT CREAM

330g milk
seeds from 1 vanilla bean
80g superfine sugar
pinch of salt
3 egg yolks
40g cornstarch
4 sheets of gelatin
500g whipping cream

FOR THE PASTRY LAYERS

275g premade chilled puff pastry, about 9½ × 16 in (24 × 40 cm)
powdered sugar for dusting

FOR THE CREAM Bring the milk to a boil in a saucepan with the vanilla, superfine sugar, and salt. Add the egg yolks and cornstarch to a bowl and combine well. Then add a small amount of boiled milk to the yolk mixture and stir until smooth to bring the mixture to temperature and dissolve any lumps of cornstarch. Add this mixture to the saucepan and cook over moderate heat for 2–3 minutes, stirring constantly, until it thickens visibly and has a lovely glossy sheen. Transfer the vanilla cream into a bowl, cover the surface with plastic wrap (the plastic wrap and cream should be touching to prevent a skin from forming) and refrigerate for 3–4 hours.

FOR THE PASTRY LAYERS Line a baking sheet with parchment paper, place the puff pastry on it, and prick it with a fork to avoid bubbles forming in the pastry during baking. Let relax at room temperature for at least 1 hour to help the pastry keep its shape when it is baked.

Preheat the oven to 400°F (200°C).

Bake the puff pastry on the middle shelf of the oven for 25–30 minutes until crisp and brown. While it is still hot, dust the pastry evenly with powdered sugar and bake on the top oven shelf until the sugar starts to caramelize (2–3 minutes). Leave the puff pastry on the baking sheet until it has cooled completely.

→

TO FINISH MAKING THE CREAM Soak the gelatin in cold water for about 5 minutes. Squeeze out the gelatin, then slowly dissolve it in 4 tablespoons of the whipping cream in a small saucepan over low heat. Let cool slightly. Whisk the remaining whipping cream until stiff. Pass the cold vanilla cream through a fine mesh strainer or process using an immersion blender, then stir in the gelatin mixture and fold in the whipped cream. Transfer to a piping bag with a ⅜-in (8-mm) round nozzle.

Cut the puff pastry sheet lengthwise into four equal-width strips. Next, slice each strip crosswise into thirds to create a total of twelve small rectangular pieces. Cover one pastry rectangle with dollops of cream. Place a second pastry rectangle on top so it is neatly aligned, and press down slightly. Then top this with dollops of the vanilla cream. Put a third pastry rectangle on top of the cream, with the side that was uppermost during baking facing up, and press gently into place. Assemble the other three cream slices in the same way. Dust with powdered sugar to serve.

Miß Wanda Schnitten.

Aus Blätterteig Streifen gebacken, mit Vanille-creme füllen, obenauf dann mit weißer Glasur überzogen mit halbierten weißen Mandeln bestreuen.

Esterházy Slice

The Esterházy slice is a Hungarian cream cake. It was developed by Budapest confectioners in the early 20th century during the Austro-Hungarian Empire and is still much loved today, mainly in Hungary and Austria but also in Germany. It is always decorated with the typical Esterházy pattern of fondant and chocolate.

For 7 slices

FOR THE JAPONAISE CAKE

160g egg whites, at room temperature (from 5–6 eggs)
160g superfine sugar
pinch of salt
160g ground almonds
pinch of ground cinnamon

FOR THE CREAM FILLING

300g milk
3 egg yolks
40g cornstarch
1 vanilla bean
150g superfine sugar
100g chocolate hazelnut spread
300g butter

TO ASSEMBLE

1 tbsp apricot jam (see p.207)
20g water
100g powdered sugar
25g dark chocolate
100g sliced almonds

Preheat the oven to 375°F (190°C). Line a 13 × 18 in (30 × 40 cm) baking sheet with parchment paper.

FOR THE JAPONAISE CAKE Beat the egg whites, sugar, and salt in a scrupulously clean bowl until stiff. Carefully fold in the almonds and cinnamon. Spread the mixture out on the lined baking sheet and smooth it out with an angled palette knife. Bake on the middle shelf of the oven for about 20 minutes until pale in color.

Let it cool down slightly, then gently pull the parchment paper off the warm base. Don't worry if it breaks because the layers can easily be reassembled later. Now cut the base lengthwise into four equal-width strips.

FOR THE CREAM FILLING Combine 3 tablespoons of milk with the egg yolks and cornstarch in a small bowl, and stir until smooth. Slice the vanilla bean in half lengthwise and scrape out the seeds with a small, sharp knife. Put the vanilla bean and seeds in a saucepan with the remaining milk and the sugar and bring to a simmer. As soon as the milk begins to boil, add 3 tablespoons of the hot milk to the cornstarch and egg yolks to bring this up to temperature. Then put everything in the saucepan and continue cooking, stirring with a balloon whisk until the mixture begins to thicken to a custard consistency. Fold in the chocolate hazelnut spread. Transfer the mixture to a bowl, cover the surface with plastic wrap, and let cool (the plastic wrap should be in contact with the surface of the custard to prevent a skin from forming).

→

Pass the cooled mixture through a fine mesh strainer or process with an immersion blender. Cream the butter in the bowl of a stand mixer with a balloon whisk attachment for 10 minutes until pale and fluffy, then stir in the custard by the spoonful.

TO ASSEMBLE Place one strip of cake on a cake plate or board and top with one-third of the cream. Place another cake strip on top of the cream and cover this with one-third of the cream in the same way. Repeat this process once more. Place the final cake strip on top and brush with the apricot jam. Let set in the fridge for about 2 hours.

Heat the water to about 149°F (65°C) on a candy thermometer. Add the powdered sugar and stir until smooth. Roughly chop the chocolate and melt it in a metal bowl over a pan of hot water. Put the melted chocolate in a disposable piping bag and cut off a small corner to create a very small hole.

Take the layered cakes out of the fridge and cover with the icing. Pipe thin, parallel lines of dark chocolate across the cake. Immediately pull a wooden skewer through the chocolate lines at right angles in alternating directions.

Put the cake in the freezer briefly so it is easier to slice into smooth pieces. To do this, first trim the edges very finely using a serrated knife. Then cut the cake into seven slices.

Toast the sliced almonds in a dry pan until golden brown, then allow to cool. Decorate the sides of the Esterházy slices with the almonds.

Esterhaszi Schnitten

18 Loth Zucker in 8 Eiweiß Schnee einschlagen, 18 Loth gebrannte Grillaschmandeln, mischen ein Blech backen, in Streifen schneiden, mit Buttercreme gefüllt weiß überziehen, von Chocolade ein Gitter spritzen.

KAFFEE ALT WIEN
KAFFEE ALT WIEN
ALT WIEN
KAFFEE ALT WIEN

Coffee Cream Roulade

Sometimes all it takes to completely unwind is an enticing coffee cream rolled up in a delicate sponge. Instead of chocolate hazelnut spread, some melted dark chocolate and a dash of finely grated orange zest also tastes great.

For 1 roulade

FOR THE SPONGE

4 eggs
pinch of salt
50g superfine sugar
2 tsp finely grated organic lemon zest
50g powdered sugar, plus extra for dusting
80g type 00 flour
20g cornstarch

FOR THE COFFEE MERINGUE CREAM

3 tsp instant coffee
4 tsp hot water
120g egg whites at room temperature (from about 4 eggs)
pinch of salt
180g superfine sugar
360g butter, at room temperature
2–3 tsp chocolate hazelnut spread

TO DECORATE

handful of chocolate-covered coffee beans

FOR THE SPONGE Preheat the oven to 350°F (180°C). Line a 13 × 18 in (30 × 40 cm) baking sheet with parchment paper.

Separate the eggs. Whisk the egg whites with the salt, sugar, and lemon zest in a scrupulously clean bowl until stiff. Whisk the egg yolks and powdered sugar in the bowl of a stand mixer for 8 minutes until light and fluffy. Sift the flour and cornstarch in a bowl, then carefully add them to the yolk mixture in batches, alternating with the egg whites, until everything is well combined.

Spread the sponge mixture on the lined baking sheet and bake on the middle shelf of the oven for 15–20 minutes. Remove the sponge from the oven and transfer it, along with the parchment paper, onto another sheet of parchment paper or a clean dish towel that has been sprinkled with powdered sugar. Carefully peel off the parchment paper that was used in the oven. Then roll up the sponge, along with the new parchment paper underneath it, and let cool down completely.

FOR THE COFFEE MERINGUE CREAM Stir the instant coffee into the hot water and let cool. Use a hand mixer to beat the egg whites, salt, and sugar in a scrupulously clean bowl over hot water until the sugar has dissolved completely. Continue whisking the mixture in a stand mixer (using the balloon whisk attachment) for 20 minutes until it is meringue consistency.

Now gradually add the very soft butter. (After adding about half the butter, the meringue will look like it has collapsed—that's normal. Just keep whisking, add the remaining butter and let the stand mixer run until the meringue is nice and creamy again.) Add the chocolate hazelnut spread and cold coffee; stir in slowly.

Carefully unroll the sponge and peel off the parchment. Spread half the coffee meringue cream over the sponge, roll it up again, and refrigerate for 1 hour. Put the remaining coffee meringue cream in a piping bag fitted with a flat, serrated nozzle and pipe it decoratively onto the roulade. Decorate with the coffee beans.

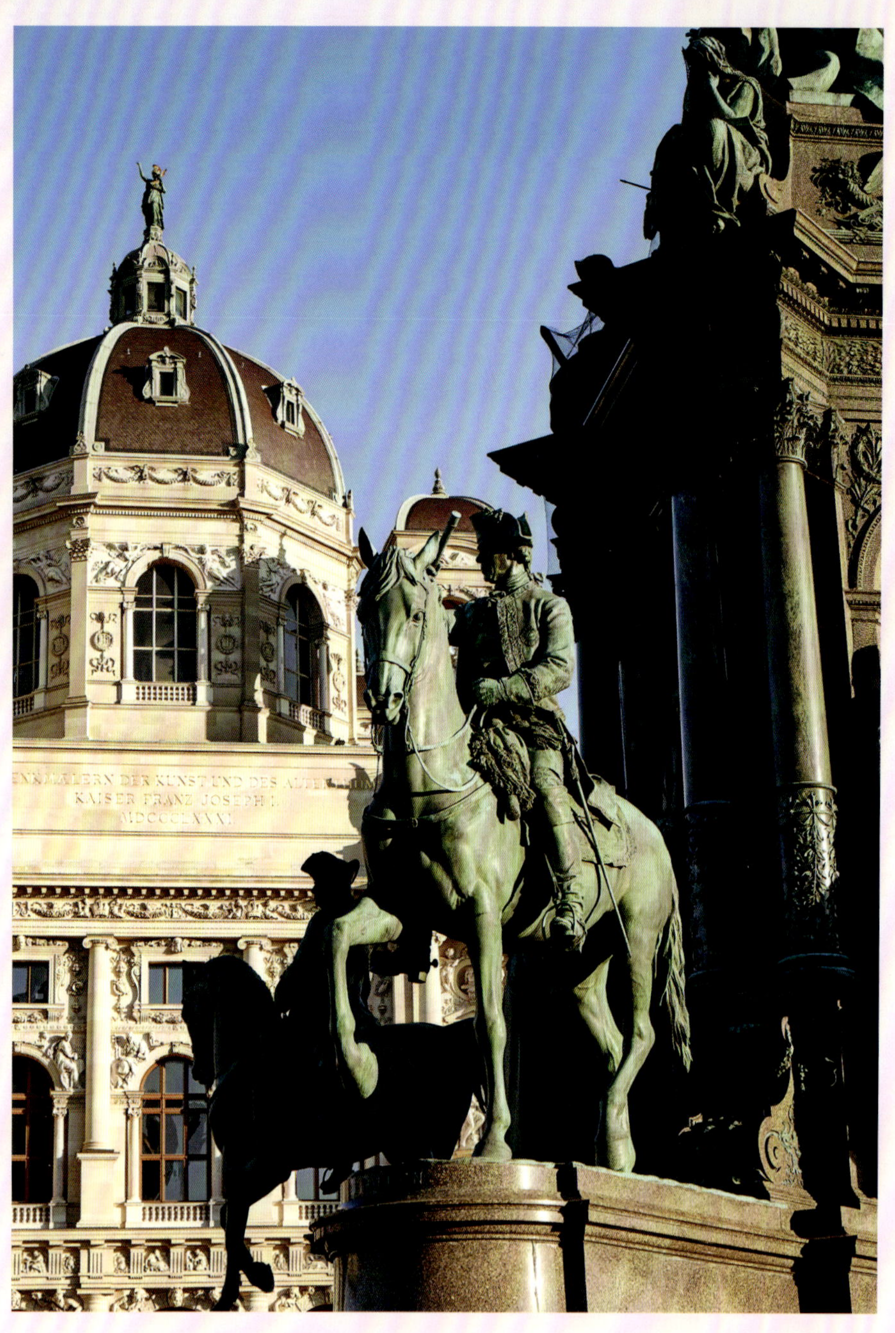

St. Stephen's Cathedral in Vienna—or *Steffl* as it is known locally—soars into the sky like an elaborately decorated meringue and cream cake.

Kardinalschnitte

The "Cardinal Slice" is a fabulous fusion of sponge and meringue and is said to have made its first appearance in 1933 in the Viennese patisserie L. Heiner for the festival known as Katholikentag *(Catholic Day). The cake features a sweet and sour red currant jam and is filled with light and airy whipped cream. The different components are said to evoke the colors of the Vatican (white and yellow) and the eminence and esteem of the cardinal (red).*

For 8 slices

FOR THE MERINGUE

90g egg whites at room temperature (from about 3 eggs)
70g superfine sugar
10g cornstarch

FOR THE SPONGE

3 egg yolks
1 egg
30g powdered sugar
1 tsp vanilla sugar (see p.200)
½ tsp finely grated organic lemon zest
pinch of salt
15g cornstarch

FOR THE FILLING

500g whipping cream
20g powdered sugar, plus extra for dusting
100g red currant jam (see p.208)

Preheat the oven to 350°F (170°C). Cut a sheet of parchment paper lengthwise into two strips about 6 in (15 cm) wide. Brush a baking sheet with a little water (this helps keep the parchment flat) and place the cut strips of parchment paper on top.

FOR THE MERINGUE Beat the egg whites and sugar in the scrupulously clean bowl of a stand mixer for about 10 minutes until creamy. Carefully fold in the cornstarch. Transfer the meringue into a piping bag with a ½-in (1-cm) round nozzle. Pipe three cylinders of meringue on each piece of parchment paper, with a gap of about ¾ in (2 cm) in between.

FOR THE SPONGE Whisk the egg yolks, egg, powdered sugar, vanilla sugar, lemon zest, and salt in a bowl for 8 minutes until creamy. Add the cornstarch and continue whisking until the mixture is pale and creamy. Put the sponge cake mixture into a second piping bag fitted with a round nozzle and pipe this into the gaps between the strips of meringue. This creates two sponge and meringue pieces, each consisting of three strips of meringue and two of sponge. Sift over some powdered sugar and bake on the middle shelf of the oven for 18–20 minutes.

Let the sponge and meringue sections cool down a little on the baking sheet, then turn them out onto a piece of parchment paper that has been sprinkled with powdered sugar, and carefully peel off the parchment that was used in the oven. Carefully turn the cakes over and let them cool down completely.

FOR THE FILLING Beat the whipping cream with the powdered sugar until stiff. Spread the jam on the bottom of each piece of sponge and meringue. Spread the whipped cream over the layer of jam on one piece and place the second sponge and meringue piece on top, jam-side down. Make sure the two pieces are aligned as precisely as possible. Cut the cake into slices and serve dusted with powdered sugar.

Swiss Roll

Swiss Roll was the first dessert I was allowed to bake independently in my grandmother's kitchen. This jam-filled classic was a regular coffee-time treat for the Wörndl family. On Mother's Day, it was traditionally filled with whipped cream and strawberries. Sometimes we even enjoyed it with crème pâtissière.

For 1 Swiss Roll

FOR THE SPONGE

6 eggs
pinch of salt
50g superfine sugar
100g powdered sugar, plus extra for dusting
150g type 00 flour

FOR THE FILLING

250g apricot jam *(see p.207)*

Preheat the oven to 350°F (180°C). Line a 13 × 18 in (30 × 40 cm) baking sheet with parchment paper.

FOR THE SPONGE Separate the eggs. Whisk the egg whites, salt, and superfine sugar in a scrupulously clean bowl until stiff. Whisk the egg yolks and powdered sugar in the bowl of a stand mixer for 8 minutes until light and fluffy.

Sift the flour into a bowl and carefully add it to the egg yolk mixture in batches, alternating with the egg whites, until everything is well combined. Spread the sponge mixture on the lined baking sheet and bake on the middle shelf of the oven for 15–20 minutes.

Remove the sponge from the oven and transfer it, along with the parchment paper, onto another sheet of parchment paper or a clean dish towel that has been sprinkled with powdered sugar. Carefully peel off the parchment paper that was used in the oven. Then roll up the sponge along with the new parchment paper underneath it and let cool down completely.

FOR THE FILLING Carefully unroll the roulade and peel off the parchment paper. Spread the sponge with apricot jam and roll it up again. Dust with powdered sugar and cut into slices.

Biesquitt Roulard

Man rührt 1/2 Pfund Zucker, 16 Dotter gut ab, 8 Eiweiß Schnee 12 Loth Mehl vermischt auf ein Blech gebacken mit Marillen bestreichen zusammenrollen, weiß überziehen.

How to make ...

Sponge

Sponge is a light and airy cake made from flour, sugar, and eggs. It is used for lots of different baked items, such as roulades, layer cakes, or cream-filled slices.

Sometimes melted butter, water, or milk is added to the sponge.

The essentials

SEPARATING THE EGGS—YES OR NO?

Whatever kind of sponge you are making, the one constant feature is that the mixture must be whipped until it is very pale and creamy. Other than that, it is entirely up to you whether to use a stand mixer or handheld electric mixer. For a sponge made with whole eggs, these are beaten with the sugar for a very long time until the mixture is nice and fluffy. That is why a stand mixer is ideal here.

For a sponge made with separated eggs, it is vital to get perfectly whipped egg whites. Make sure the eggs are separated cleanly. The bowl and whisk must be scrupulously clean to achieve a stiff consistency. The egg whites are ready when they form peaks and the bowl could theoretically be turned upside down without anything coming out.

SIFT THEN FOLD IN THE FLOUR

It is essential to sift the flour and baking powder (and cornstarch if applicable) to avoid any little lumps forming. The flour mixture must be carefully folded in using a spatula. Otherwise, the air will be knocked out of the beaten eggs and the cake will not rise properly or achieve a light and airy texture.

TESTING WITH A SKEWER

When making a sponge it is a good idea to test with a skewer to check that it is done (see p.30).

Variations

You can create a chocolate version by replacing 10–20g of the flour with the same quantity of cocoa powder. Different flavors can be achieved using vanilla, orange or lemon zest, and spices.

If the middle of the cake bulges upward, the oven temperature was probably too high. The sponge can be rescued by turning it out of the pan after baking and letting it cool upside down.

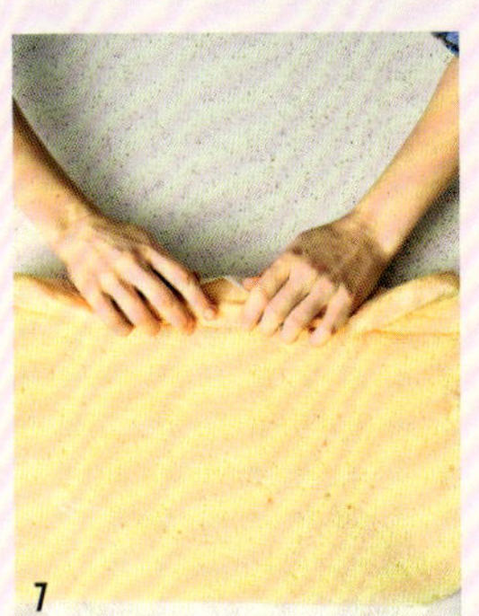

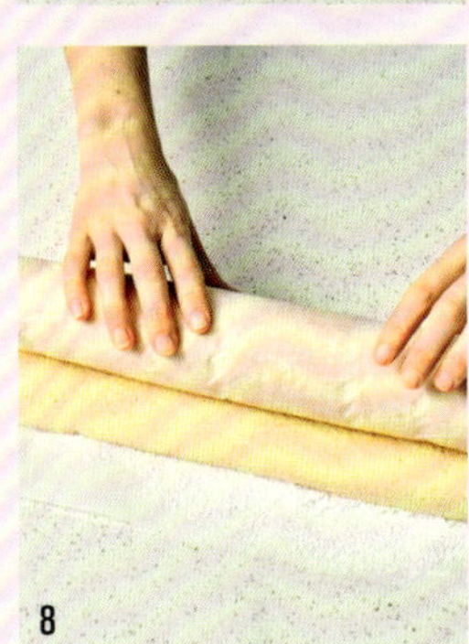

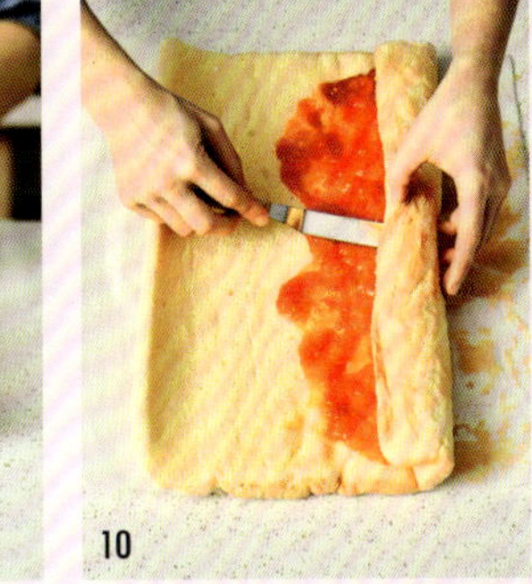

1. Add the yolk mixture to the whisked egg whites.

2. Carefully fold it in.

3. Sift the flour and fold this in carefully too.

4. Transfer the sponge mix onto the prepared tray.

5. Spread it out using an angled palette knife.

6. Tip the cooked sponge out onto another sheet of parchment paper and pull off the top sheet.

7.+8. Quickly roll up the sponge along with the bottom sheet of parchment to make a roulade, and let cool.

9. Carefully unroll the roulade.

10. Spread the sponge with jam.

11. Roll up the roulade again, this time without the parchment paper.

12. Dust with powdered sugar to serve.

Afternoon Tea

Afternoon tea or coffee is another very important part of life in Vienna. The locals call this a *Kaffejause*, which combines the word for coffee with the word for a snack or light meal. And it is timed for exactly the point when people are in the depths of the afternoon slump. The more you think about it, the more you crave a *Kleiner Brauner* (espresso with a splash of milk) and a bite of something sweet to keep you going. Whether it's delicious little Butter Cookies (see p.121), a Striezel (sweet braided bread, see p.106), or a Punschkrapferl (bright pink iced cake, see p.124)—anything goes, as long as it boosts the spirits.

Cream Horns

In Vienna these delicious cream-filled pastries are called Schaumrollen *and they are an essential feature of any traditional fair or Christmas market. A visit to Vienna's Prater Park is unthinkable without a* Schaumrolle.

For 12 cream horns

FOR THE CRISP BUTTER PASTRY

225g type 00 flour, plus extra for the work surface
1 tbsp superfine sugar
2g salt
150g cold butter
75g very cold water

FOR BRUSHING AND DUSTING

1 egg
pinch of salt
1 tbsp whipping cream
powdered sugar

FOR THE MERINGUE

60g egg whites at room temperature (from about 2 eggs)
pinch of salt
60g powdered sugar
60g superfine sugar

FOR THE PASTRY Combine the flour, sugar, and salt and create a mound on the work surface. Dice the butter and roughly work it into the flour with a dough scraper, then crumble the mixture between your fingertips so some larger pieces of butter remain. Work in the water, press the pastry together (do not knead), wrap in plastic wrap, and refrigerate for at least 1 hour.

Roll out the pastry on a floured work surface to about 6 x 12 in (15 × 30 cm). Fold it twice to create three layers, one on top of the other (like a letter). Turn the dough 90 degrees, then roll and fold it again as just described. Lightly press the layers with the rolling pin, wrap in plastic wrap, and refrigerate for at least 1 hour.

Preheat the oven to 400°F (200°C). Line a baking sheet with parchment paper.

FOR BRUSHING Separate the egg. Mix the egg white with salt and the yolk with cream. Roll out the pastry on a floured work surface until it is about ⅛ in (3 mm) thick and about 10 x 14 in (25 × 35 cm) in size. Cut it lengthwise into strips about ¾ in (2 cm) wide. Brush with the egg white, leaving the edges free. With the brushed side facing outward, wrap each strip in an overlapping spiral shape around special cream horn molds, diameter about ½ in (1.3 cm), then brush each one with the yolk mixture. Place these with the end facing down and about ¾ in (2 cm) apart on the lined baking sheet and bake on the middle shelf of the oven for 12–15 minutes until light brown. Carefully release the pastries from the molds and allow to cool completely.

FOR THE MERINGUE Use a hand mixer to beat the egg whites, salt, and both sugars in a scrupulously clean bowl over a pan of hot water until the sugar has dissolved. Continue whisking in a stand mixer (using the balloon whisk attachment) for 10–15 minutes until it reaches meringue consistency.

Transfer the meringue mixture into a piping bag with a nozzle suitable for the opening in the cream horns, and pipe in the mixture from both sides. Dust with powdered sugar.

Linz Cookies

These cookies are named after the town of Linz and are closely related to the traditional Austrian Spitzbuben (see p.192). No bakery is complete without them, and they are always in season. Thanks to their similarity to the Christmas specialty Spitzbuben, they bring a festive feel to any coffee break, whatever the time of year.

For 30–40 cookies

FOR THE COOKIE DOUGH

150g cold butter
200g type 00 flour, plus extra for the work surface
100g ground blanched almonds
100g powdered sugar, plus extra for dusting
seeds from ½ vanilla bean
½ tsp finely grated organic lemon zest
1 egg
pinch of salt

FOR THE FILLING

½ tsp rum
250g strained jam of your choice (see pp.207–209)

FOR THE DOUGH Cut the butter into cubes. Use your fingertips to rub it into the flour, almonds, powdered sugar, and vanilla. Add the remaining ingredients and work everything swiftly together until you have a smooth dough. Wrap in plastic wrap and refrigerate for about 1 hour.

Preheat the oven to 350°F (180°C). Line a baking sheet with parchment paper.

Roll out the cookie dough on a floured work surface until it is about 1/16–1/8 in (2–3 mm) thick, then stamp out circles. In half of these shapes, also stamp out a smaller circle to make the typical hole in the center. Place all the cookie circles about ¾ in (2 cm) apart on the lined baking sheet. Combine the leftover cookie dough and repeat the steps above. Bake the cookies for 8–10 minutes on the middle shelf of the oven until golden, then let cool.

FOR THE FILLING Heat the rum and jam in a small pan. Take the cookies without holes and spread jam onto the side that was facing down during baking. Dust the cookies with the holes with powdered sugar and place them on the jam-covered bases.

184
al - ler Pracht;
es rie-se
71
der Him-mel ist blau!
Laßt
riten.
breit, wie im Anfang
poco a poco cresc.
r. H.
sol - len froh - lok
nah;
läu - ten
ken: Der Lenz
ist
U. E. 3700.

Austrian Hausfreunde

Sweet treats that quickly fill up a big cookie jar really are the perfect "house friends," as the name of these Austrian cookies suggests. And the dried fruit and nuts in this recipe can be varied depending on what ingredients you have on hand. That's another friendly feature of these cookies.

For about 50

FOR THE COOKIE DOUGH

80g mixed candied citrus fruits (e.g. lemons, oranges, grapefruit)
80g raisins
50g rum
100g hazelnuts
100g dark chocolate (at least 65 percent cocoa)
1 tsp aniseed
2 eggs
120g superfine sugar
seeds from ½ vanilla bean
220g type 00 flour, plus extra for the work surface
1 tsp baking powder

TO DECORATE (OPTIONAL)

150g dark chocolate
citrus zest

FOR THE COOKIE DOUGH Roughly chop the candied citrus fruits, add the raisins, and infuse in the rum for about 1 hour.

Preheat the oven to 350°F (180°C). Line a baking sheet with parchment paper.

Roughly chop the hazelnuts and chocolate. Drain the candied fruit and mix well with the hazelnuts and chocolate in a bowl. Slightly crush the aniseed using a pestle and mortar, but do not grind too finely.

Whisk the eggs, sugar, vanilla, and aniseed in a bowl until light and fluffy. Sift the flour and baking powder into a bowl and fold this into the egg mixture along with the drained candied fruits, nuts, and chocolate. Use a dough scraper to get the dough out of the bowl and onto a floured work surface. Divide the dough in half and shape each piece into a log. Place both logs on the lined baking sheet and bake on the middle shelf of the oven for about 20 minutes.

While the dough is still warm, cut it into slices about ½ in (1 cm) thick and let cool.

TO DECORATE If you would like to decorate them, roughly chop the chocolate and melt it in a metal bowl over a pan of hot water. Dip the cookies into the melted chocolate to coat them as desired. Decorate with citrus zest, then let dry on a sheet of parchment paper.

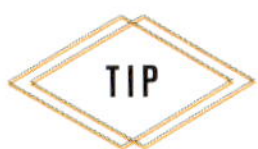

If you prefer an even crunchier texture, you can follow the same technique that is used for *cantucci*, the Italian cousins of these cookies. This involves baking the cookies for a second time after they are cut from the log, using the same oven temperature and allowing them to turn golden brown.

Striezel

Austrian Striezel is a sweet, braided bread that is also known as Butterzopf *or* Osterzopf *(butter or Easter braid). On All Saints' Day, Austrian godparents give their godchildren a Striezel as a sign of their loyal bond. Sometimes, a coin is even baked into the loaf as a little gift.*

For 1 loaf

FOR THE YEAST DOUGH

90g butter

190g milk

500g all-purpose flour, plus extra for working

7g salt

75g superfine sugar

2 egg yolks

25g fresh yeast (see p.110 for converting to dried)

finely grated zest of ½ organic orange

finely grated zest of ½ organic lemon

FOR BRUSHING

1 egg yolk

25g whipping cream

FOR THE DOUGH Melt the butter over low heat. Add the milk. Put the remaining ingredients in the bowl of a stand mixer, add the butter and milk, and (using the dough hook attachment) knead on the lowest setting for 5 minutes. Let rest for 3 minutes, then knead again on a medium setting for 10 minutes. Shape the dough into a ball, cover with plastic wrap, and let rise in a warm place for 1½–2 hours.

Divide the dough into three, four, or six pieces of equal weight on a floured work surface. Shape into balls, cover with plastic wrap, and let rise in a warm place for 10–15 minutes.

Line a baking sheet with parchment paper.

Shape the balls of dough into uniform strands. Lightly flour these strands of dough then create a braid consisting of three, four, or six strands. Tuck the ends of the dough underneath.

Transfer the Striezel onto the lined baking sheet, cover with plastic wrap, and let rise in a warm place for about 1 hour.

Preheat the oven to 350°F (180°C).

FOR BRUSHING Whisk the egg yolk and whipping cream and brush onto the Striezel. Bake on the middle shelf of the oven for about 50 minutes. To make completely sure the bread is cooked, check the internal temperature using a kitchen thermometer: 201°F (94°C) is perfect. Finally, let cool on a wire rack.

Milk Loaf

The eggs give this loaf a beautiful golden color. But since items baked with eggs can dry out more easily, a cooked flour paste and a sourdough starter are used to ensure the necessary fluffy texture. If baking using wild fermentation isn't your thing, you will still be thrilled with the pure yeast version.

FOR THE COOKED FLOUR PASTE The day before you intend to bake, bring the milk and flour to a boil, stirring constantly. Transfer to a bowl, cover with plastic wrap, and transfer to the fridge to cool completely.

FOR THE YEAST DOUGH Put all the ingredients except the butter in the bowl of a stand mixer, add the cooked flour paste, and (using the dough hook attachment) knead the dough on a low setting for 4–5 minutes. Scrape the dough away from the sides of the bowl with a dough spatula and continue kneading for 10 minutes on a medium setting. With the machine still running, gradually add the butter and continue kneading for 5–7 minutes until it has been well incorporated into the dough. Cover the dough with plastic wrap and let rise for about 1 hour in a warm place.

After 1 hour, fold the dough for the first time as follows: with a damp hand, reach under the dough in the bowl, carefully pull it up slightly then place it down on the opposite side. Turn the bowl 90 degrees three times, repeating the folding process on each quarter turn. After a further 2 hours proving time, fold the dough again as just described. Cover with plastic wrap and let rise in the fridge for about 12 hours.

The next day, grease a 12-in (30-cm) loaf pan with butter and line with parchment paper. Divide the dough into six equal pieces on a floured work surface and shape into balls. Place the balls of dough snugly together in two rows in the loaf pan, cover with plastic wrap, and let rise for 2½–3 hours in a warm place. The dough should have risen well; if you shake the pan, the dough should wobble a bit like a custard.

Preheat the oven to 350°F (180°C).

FOR BRUSHING Whisk the egg yolk, salt, and milk; brush onto the dough. Bake on the middle shelf of the oven for 45–50 minutes until golden. Check the internal temperature with a kitchen thermometer: 201°F (94°C) is perfect. Let cool in the pan.

For 1 loaf

FOR THE COOKED FLOUR PASTE

125g milk
25g all-purpose flour

FOR THE YEAST DOUGH

380g all-purpose flour, plus extra for the work surface
40g milk
90g ripe sourdough starter (alternatively use a total of 18g fresh yeast or see p.110 for converting to dried)
10g fresh yeast (see p.110 for converting to dried)
25g superfine sugar
40g honey
10g salt
3 eggs
125g butter, at room temperature

FOR BRUSHING

1 egg
pinch of salt
1 tsp milk

How to make ...

Yeast dough

Yeast doughs are made from flour, water, yeast, and salt. Depending on the type of item being baked, other ingredients such as sugar, butter, eggs, or milk may be used.

The essentials

TIME

Yeast doughs require time (depending on how much yeast is added in the recipe) and must be left to rest to achieve the best results. This ensures a silky smooth texture.

FRESH OR DRIED YEAST?

Yeast is a fungus that makes the dough rise. You can get fresh or dried yeast. Great results can be achieved with either option. Fresh yeast can easily be replaced by dry yeast as follows:

1 cube (42g) fresh yeast =
2 packets (14g) dried yeast

Kneading the dough

It is important to knead yeast doughs long enough to ensure they are stretchy, malleable, and stable. This may well take 10 minutes. The dough will then be given enough time to rise when it is left to rest.

Leaving the dough to rest

After kneading, the dough should always be covered with plastic wrap and put in a warm place at 79–81°F (26–27°C) to rest (and rise). The warm place will vary depending on the season and your particular domestic setting. It might be somewhere near a heating vent or coffee machine, or a stove where something is simmering.

Variations

Yeast doughs can be refined with all sorts of different ingredients, for example with nuts, dried fruits, chocolate, spices, or citrus zest.

- While it is true that yeast doughs love warmth, you can achieve a particularly light texture in the fridge—if you give the dough a long time to rise, for example overnight.
- The "windowpane" test is a very reliable way to tell whether the dough has been kneaded long enough. You should be able to gently stretch the dough so your fingers are visible through it. If the dough tears before this is possible, it has not yet been kneaded sufficiently. This test is mainly used for dough that is high in wheat. Skip this test for doughs containing lots of rye or spelt flour.

1. Knead all the ingredients into a smooth dough.

2. Shape the dough into a ball.

3. Folding: with a moistened hand, reach under the dough in the bowl, and carefully pull it up slightly.

4. Place the section of dough you have lifted back down on the opposite side.

5. Turn the bowl 90 degrees three times, repeating the folding process on each quarter turn.

6. Cover the dough with plastic wrap to rise.

7. Knock the dough back after proving.

8. Divide the dough into equal pieces.

9. Shape the pieces of dough into balls to be used as desired.

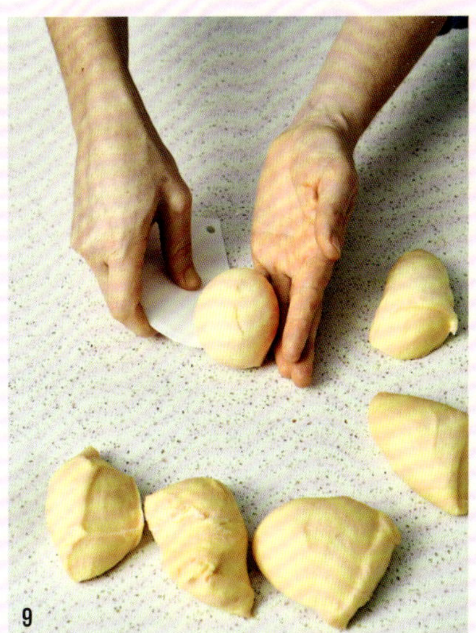

Brioche

The aroma of freshly baked brioche is simply irresistible. You might enjoy yours with jam and butter for breakfast, or lightly toasted and dunked in a delicious stew, or perhaps as the base for scrambled eggs or sandwiches. If you happen to have any leftovers, you can make excellent croutons for salads and soups.

For 1 brioche

FOR THE YEAST DOUGH

390g all-purpose flour, plus extra for the pan and work surface
30g superfine sugar
20g honey
40g milk
90g buttermilk
3 egg yolks
2 eggs
10g fresh yeast (see p.110 for converting to dried)
8g salt
130g butter, at room temperature, plus extra for greasing

FOR BRUSHING

1 egg yolk
2 tbsp whipping cream
pinch of salt

FOR THE DOUGH Knead all the ingredients except the butter in the bowl of a stand mixer (using the dough hook attachment) for 3 minutes on a low setting. Knead for 5 minutes on a medium setting until you have a smooth and elastic dough. With the processor still running, add the butter in pieces and continue kneading for another 5 minutes. Cover with plastic wrap and let rise for about 1 hour in a warm place.

Grease a 9-in (22-cm) brioche pan or a high-sided springform pan with butter and dust with flour. Knead the dough once again and divide it into six equal pieces. Cover the dough and let it relax for 10–15 minutes. Then shape the pieces of dough into balls on a floured work surface and place five of them in the pan with seams facing down. Place the sixth ball on top, also with seam facing down. Cover and let rise for 1–1½ hours. The dough should have risen well; if you shake the pan, the dough should wobble a bit like a custard.

Preheat the oven to 400°F (200°C).

FOR BRUSHING Whisk the egg yolk, whipping cream, and salt, and brush onto the dough. Place the brioche on the lowest shelf in the oven, reduce the temperature to 350°F (180°C) and bake the brioche for 40–50 minutes until golden brown. To make completely sure the brioche is cooked, check the internal temperature using a kitchen thermometer: 201°F (94°C) is perfect. Let the brioche cool. Remove it from the pan and enjoy with butter while as fresh as possible.

The dough can also be left in the fridge to rise for 10–12 hours after kneading. The next day, divide the cold dough into pieces as described above, shape each piece into a ball, place them in the pan, and allow to rise for about 4 hours.

Crescent Rolls

These crescent rolls—or Mürbe Kipferl *as they are known—are an absolute breakfast classic in Vienna's cafés. They are said to have been invented by the baking couple Peter and Eva Wendler, who were inspired by the shape of the Turkish crescent during the Ottoman sieges of Vienna. But then again, others insist that these rolls were a familiar pagan tradition well before this period. Today, the crescent rolls are also regarded as a symbol for sharing, so children share* Kipferl *every year to celebrate Saint Martin's Day.*

For 10 crescents

FOR THE YEAST DOUGH

500g all-purpose flour
50g superfine sugar
150g milk
120g water
50g butter, at room temperature
10g salt
10g roasted barley malt flour
6g fresh yeast (see p.110 for converting to dried)

FOR THE DOUGH The day before baking, knead all the ingredients in the bowl of a stand mixer (using the dough hook attachment) for about 10 minutes until you have a smooth dough. Cover with plastic wrap and leave overnight to rise in the fridge for 10–12 hours.

The next day, take the dough out of the fridge about 2 hours before you are ready to start the next steps and allow it to rest.

Divide the dough into ten equal pieces and shape into balls. Cover and let rest in a warm place for about 20 minutes. Line a baking sheet with parchment paper.

Press the dough balls slightly flat with your hand and roll them out into flat oval disks about 10 in (25 cm) in length. Now roll up the dough with the flat of your hand, applying a little pressure as you do so, and pulling the lower end of the dough slightly with your other hand. Shape these rolls into crescents and place them on the lined baking sheet, ensuring there are sufficient gaps in between. Spray the crescents with a little water, cover, and let rise in a warm place for about 1 hour.

Preheat the oven to 400°F (200°C).

Now spray the crescents liberally with water and bake on the middle shelf of the oven for about 20 minutes until golden. Let cool on a wire rack.

By leaving the dough to prove overnight and adding roasted malt, these crescent rolls acquire a particularly delicious flavor. If you want a slightly faster option, you can use 15g of fresh yeast (or see p.110 for converting to dried) and just leave the dough to rise for 1 hour before shaping. Immediately after this, shape the dough into crescents and bake as described after rising.

Mini Choux Puffs

In German, these sweet choux puffs are known as Brandteigkrapferl, *which translates as "burned dough" or "scalded dough." The name comes from the way the pastry is made by heating butter, milk, and flour so that it roasts or "burns." These light and airy treats are also known as cream puffs or* pâte à choux.

For 12–14 choux puffs

FOR THE CHOUX PASTRY

70g type 00 flour
60g butter
60g water
60g milk
¼ tsp salt
1 tsp superfine sugar
110g egg, at room temperature (about 2 eggs)
powdered sugar for dusting

FOR THE VANILLA CREAM

2 egg yolks
30g cornstarch
250g milk, divided
40g superfine sugar
seeds from ½ vanilla bean
pinch of salt
250g whipping cream

FOR THE PASTRY Sift the flour twice. Bring the butter, water, milk, salt, and sugar to a boil. Remove from the heat and quickly add the flour. Stir with a wooden spoon until the dough is coming away from the sides of the pan. Return to the stove and cook for 3–5 minutes over low heat, stirring constantly.

Transfer the dough to the bowl of a stand mixer and mix for 1 minute using the paddle attachment to cool it down. Lightly whisk the eggs, and gradually work these into the dough until they have been completely absorbed. The mixture should drop gently from the mixer attachment but should not be runny. Transfer the dough to a piping bag fitted with a serrated nozzle and let rest in the fridge for 1–2 hours.

Preheat the oven to 400°F (200°C). Line a baking sheet with parchment paper.

Pipe little swirls of dough 2 in (5 cm) apart on the lined baking sheet and dust with powdered sugar. Slide the tray into the oven on the middle shelf, lower the temperature to 350°F (170°C) and bake for about 40 minutes. Do not open the oven door under any circumstances during the first 30 minutes. Leave the choux puffs on the baking sheet until completely cool.

FOR THE VANILLA CREAM Combine the egg yolks, cornstarch, and 50g of the milk. Bring the remaining 200g of milk to a boil with the sugar, vanilla, and salt. Add the egg yolk mixture, stirring constantly. Boil vigorously for a few seconds. Remove from the heat, cover the mixture with plastic wrap (the plastic should touch the surface of the custard to prevent skin from forming), and let cool. Purée or pass the mixture through a fine strainer.

Slice the choux puffs in half using a serrated knife. Whip the cream until stiff, and swiftly fold this into the cooled custard. Transfer the creamy filling into a piping bag fitted with a star nozzle and pipe onto the choux pastry bases. Put the pastry lids on top and dust with powdered sugar to serve.

The display cases in Vienna's cafés are crammed with delicious local baking specialties. They are a feast for the eyes, but the real treat is to place an order and have it whisked straight to your table.

Butter Cookies

Sometimes what you really need is a little something to nibble on alongside your afternoon tea. And that's where these delicate butter cookies are the perfect choice. They are wonderful for dunking in tea, hot chocolate, or coffee.

For about 40 cookies

FOR THE COOKIE DOUGH

110g cold butter

200g all-purpose flour, plus extra for the work surface

50g powdered sugar

some vanilla or 2 tsp vanilla sugar (see p.200)

1 tsp finely grated organic lemon zest

1 tsp finely grated organic orange zest

1 small egg or 1 medium egg yolk

pinch of salt

FOR THE COOKIE DOUGH Cut the butter into cubes. Use your fingertips to rub the butter into the flour, powdered sugar, vanilla or vanilla sugar, and citrus zests. Add the egg (or yolk) and salt and work everything swiftly together to make a smooth dough. Wrap in plastic wrap and refrigerate for about 1 hour.

Preheat the oven to 350°F (170°C). Line a baking sheet with parchment paper.

Roll out the dough on a floured work surface until it is about 1/16–1/8 in (2–3 mm) thick, then stamp out different shapes using your chosen cookie cutters. Combine the leftover cookie dough and repeat the steps above to create more shapes. Place the cookies on the lined baking sheet, ensuring there are sufficient gaps between.

Bake on the middle shelf of the oven for 10–12 minutes until pale in color. Let cool on a wire rack.

Viennese Iced Coffee

If you page through the ice cream menu in a traditional café, one thing is clear: a real Viennese iced coffee consists of black coffee, vanilla ice cream, and lots of whipped cream. A "stirred" version is also available. This refreshing beverage is said to have been served for the first time to the residents of Vienna in 1790 by a coffee roaster named Milani, who ran a little outdoor refreshment stand, a Schanigarten *as the locals call them today.*

For 1 iced coffee

50g whipping cream
2 scoops vanilla ice cream
100–150g hot or cold diluted espresso
cocoa powder and hollow wafer rolls to decorate

Whip the cream and put it in a piping bag fitted with a star nozzle. Put the scoops of vanilla ice cream into a tall glass. Pour the coffee over the ice cream and swirl the whipped cream on top. Dust with cocoa and decorate with the wafer rolls.

You can choose to make this with brewed coffee or with an intense, dark black espresso, which is then diluted with hot water. Either way, the coffee should be beautifully aromatic.

Punschkrapferl

This is an Austrian coffee house classic: an irresistible combination of chocolate, apricot jam, rum, and sponge.

For 12 little cakes

FOR THE SPONGE

30g butter
80g type 00 flour
20g cornstarch
100g superfine sugar
4 eggs
pinch of salt
1 tsp finely grated organic lemon zest

FOR THE FILLING

50g dark chocolate (at least 65 percent cocoa)
100g apricot jam (see p.207)
25–30g rum
seeds from ½ vanilla bean
juice of ½ lemon

TO ASSEMBLE

10g water
10g rum
100g powdered sugar
red food coloring
25g dark chocolate (at least 65 percent cocoa)
12 candied cherries with stems

Preheat the oven to 350°F (180°C). Line a 10-in (25-cm) square baking pan with parchment paper.

FOR THE SPONGE Melt the butter. Sift the flour and cornstarch into a bowl. Whisk the sugar, eggs, salt, and lemon zest in the bowl of a stand mixer for 7–8 minutes until creamy. Carefully fold in the flour mixture, then the butter. Spread the sponge mixture into the lined baking pan until it is about the width of a finger thick. Then bake for 12–15 minutes until golden. Turn the sponge out onto a sheet of parchment paper, remove the top piece of parchment, and let cool completely.

Lift the sponge onto a board and cut out two rectangles, 4¾ × 6¼ in (12 × 16 cm) in size. Roughly dice the leftover sponge.

FOR THE FILLING Roughly chop the chocolate and melt it in a metal bowl over a pan of hot water. Add the jam, rum, vanilla, lemon juice, and diced sponge and mix well. Transfer this mixture to a food processor and blitz until smooth.

Spread the filling evenly over one of the sponge rectangles, place the second rectangle on top, and make sure the filling is smoothed out at the edges. Weigh the cake down with a board and let stand for about 1 hour.

Place a sheet of parchment paper under a wire rack. Slice the filled sponge using a serrated knife to make twelve squares, each measuring about 1¾ in (4 cm), and place these spaced out on the wire rack.

TO ASSEMBLE Heat the water and rum to about 149°F (65°C). Add the powdered sugar and stir until smooth. Use a couple of drops of red food coloring to dye the icing pink. Pour the pink icing over the little cakes. Let the icing dry.

Roughly chop the chocolate, melt it in a metal bowl over a pan of hot water, and transfer into a disposable piping bag. Cut off a small corner of the bag to create a very small hole. Decorate the Punschkrapferl with the chocolate, and top each cake with a candied cherry.

Almond Straws

An excellent recipe to transform leftover egg whites into a heavenly light meringue treat. Delicate chocolate and flakes of sea salt add a dash of extravagance.

For 30–40

FOR THE MERINGUE

90g egg whites at room temperature (from about 3 eggs)
pinch of salt
1 tsp vanilla sugar (see p.200)
90g superfine sugar
90g powdered sugar
170g sliced almonds
pinch of ground cinnamon

TO PREPARE

4 sheets edible wafer paper, about 5 x 8 in (12 x 20 cm)
100g dark chocolate
1 tbsp coarse sea salt

FOR THE MERINGUE Use a hand mixer to beat the egg whites, salt, and all the different types of sugar in a scrupulously clean bowl over a pan of hot water until the sugar has dissolved completely. Continue whisking the mixture in a stand mixer (using the balloon whisk attachment) for 10 minutes until it reaches meringue consistency. Fold in the sliced almonds and ground cinnamon.

TO PREPARE Spread the almond meringue over the wafer paper sheets and let rest for about 30 minutes.

Preheat the oven to 350°F (180°C). Line a baking sheet with parchment paper.

Slice the meringue-topped wafer sheets into strips with a sharp knife and place on the lined baking sheet, ensuring there are sufficient gaps in between. Bake on the lowest shelf of the oven for about 15 minutes.

Roughly chop the chocolate and melt it in a metal bowl over a pan of hot water. Dip one end of each almond straw diagonally in the melted chocolate to coat. Place each straw on a wire rack or parchment paper, sprinkle with a bit of salt, and let dry.

Mandel Bogen
1 ℔ Zucker, 1 ℔ Mandl Citronenschallen,
5 Eier, dass Eiweiss zu Schnee, dass alles in
ein Schneebacken und am Feuer rühren bis
es sich von Schneebacken bis dan auf Oblatten
geben in Streifen schneiden, über Form
kühl backen

Strudels & Pastries

Strudels and pastries can be served hot or at room temperature, and are also ideal as desserts. Apple Strudel (see p.135) is probably the best known dish in this category. It tastes great slightly warm, but is equally good cold. Pancakes, Apricot Dumplings (see p.151), and Kaiserschmarren (see p.154) are not necessarily thought of as dessert in Austria, but are served at various times of day as a "sweet main course" and they are a popular choice for dinner. So, lots of children in Vienna say "Good night" with a mouthful of pancake!

Quark Strudel

Delicate, wafer-thin pastry encases a creamy filling. And since apricots and quark have always been a dream combination, the filling can also be topped with a few fruity wedges during apricot season.

For 1 strudel

FOR THE STRUDEL DOUGH

200g type 00 flour, plus extra for rolling
pinch of salt
2 tbsp oil, plus more for rubbing in
110g lukewarm water

FOR THE FILLING

50g raisins
2 tsp rum
3 eggs
120g butter, at room temperature
70g superfine sugar
seeds from ½ vanilla bean
500g full-fat quark or other curd cheese
100g sour cream or crème fraîche
juice of 1 organic lemon and 1 tsp finely grated zest
1 tbsp cornstarch
1 tbsp semolina

TO SERVE

powdered sugar for dusting

FOR THE DOUGH Work the flour, salt, oil, and water together by hand until you have a smooth, stretchy dough. Shape into a ball and rub in a few drops of oil. Place in a bowl, cover with a plate, and let rest at room temperature for about 30 minutes.

FOR THE FILLING Meanwhile, soak the raisins in the rum. Separate the eggs, and whisk the egg whites in a scrupulously clean bowl until stiff. Cream 70g of the butter with the sugar and vanilla until light and fluffy. Gradually stir in the egg yolks, quark, sour cream or crème fraîche, lemon juice and zest, cornstarch, and semolina. Carefully fold in the egg whites.

Preheat the oven to 350°F (180°C). Line a baking sheet with parchment paper.

Dust a large dish towel or tablecloth evenly with flour. Roll out the strudel dough on this cloth as thinly as possible. Then slide your flat hands under the pastry and stretch it over the backs of your hands, working from the center outward, making the pastry thinner and thinner until you can see the cloth through it. Don't worry if there are little holes here and there.

Melt the remaining 50g of butter, let it cool down slightly, then lightly brush the strudel dough with 3 tablespoons of melted butter. Spread the quark filling over the pastry, leaving a gap of about 2 in (5 cm) around the edge. Drain the rum-infused raisins and sprinkle them over the filling.

Fold in the edges of the pastry toward the middle. Using the cloth, loosely roll up the strudel from the short side and place it seam-side down on the lined baking sheet. Brush the strudel with the remaining melted butter and bake on the middle shelf of the oven for about 20 minutes. Lower the oven temperature to 300°F (150°C) and continue baking the strudel for another 10–15 minutes. Let cool slightly.

Cut the strudel into slices and serve dusted with powdered sugar.

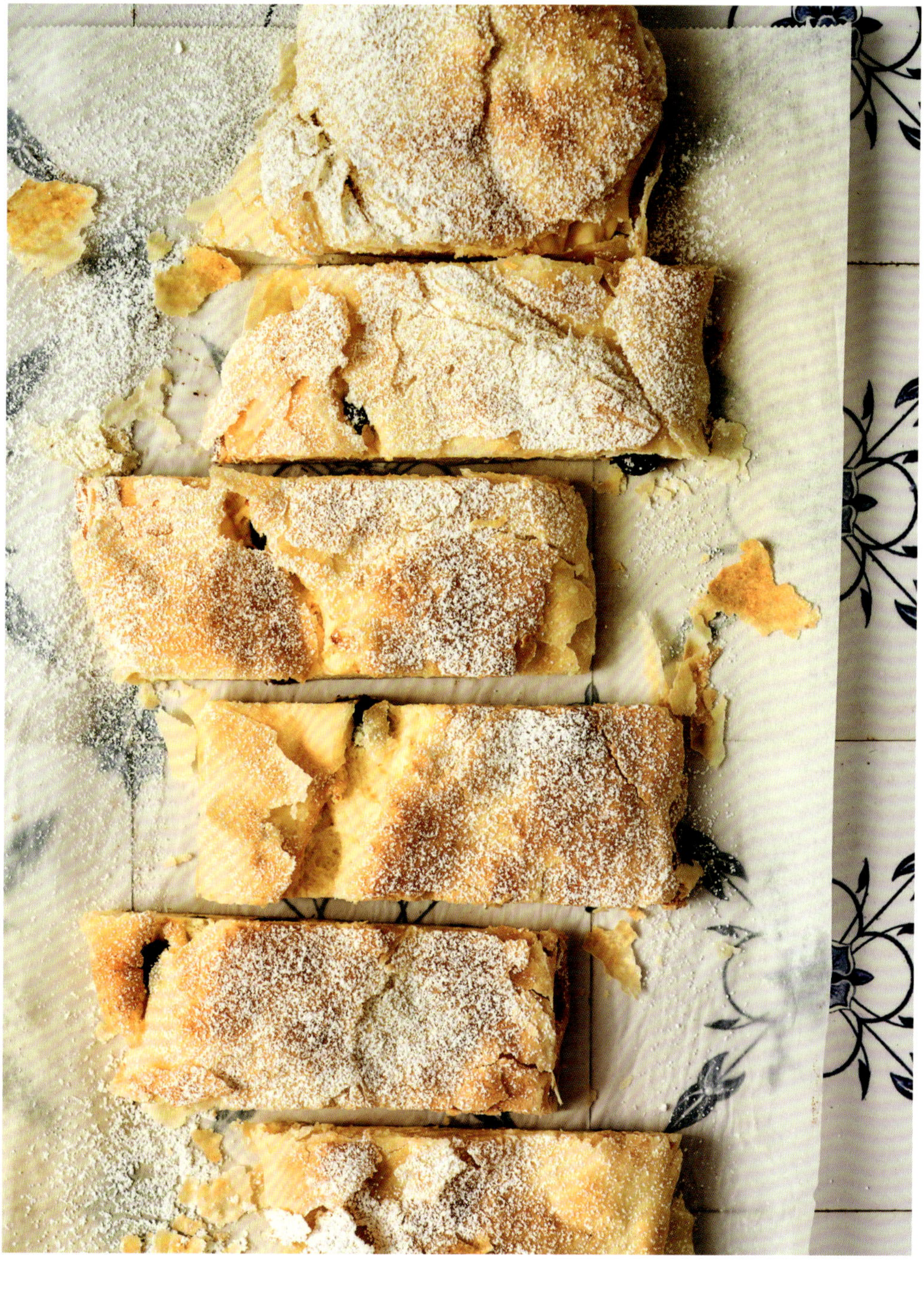

TIP

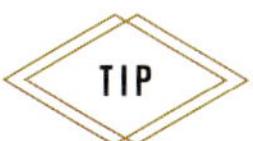

The quark strudel can also be baked in a rectangular metal roasting pan or a long casserole dish.

How to make ...

Strudel dough

Strudel dough is a thin, stretchy dough made from flour, water, salt, and oil. It has a long history dating back to the Middle Ages: the first strudels were probably made in Hungary and Romania, before gradually spreading throughout Europe.

The essentials

Resting

All the ingredients are first kneaded to create a very smooth dough, which should then be left to rest for 30 minutes. This allows the dough to relax, which makes it easier to stretch later.

Rolling and stretching

After the dough has rested, it is not kneaded again. Instead, it is immediately rolled out and then stretched. This process involves stretching and pulling the dough by hand until it is almost transparent. The thinner the pastry is, the crispier it will be once baked. In many places in Austria, there is a saying that the pastry is only thin enough when you can read a newspaper placed underneath.

Filling

Lots of different ingredients can be used as a strudel filling. The most popular choices are apples, cherries, apricots, plums, and quark or other curd cheese, such as cottage cheese, cream cheese, or mascarpone.

- The dough should be kneaded well to ensure it is smooth and stretchy. To prevent the dough from drying out while it is resting and before the stretching process, the ball of dough should be coated with a thin layer of oil.
- If a dash of vinegar is added to the dough, it will be even stretchier.
- It doesn't matter too much if the dough tears occasionally. Just press the pastry together again around the hole and continue stretching.

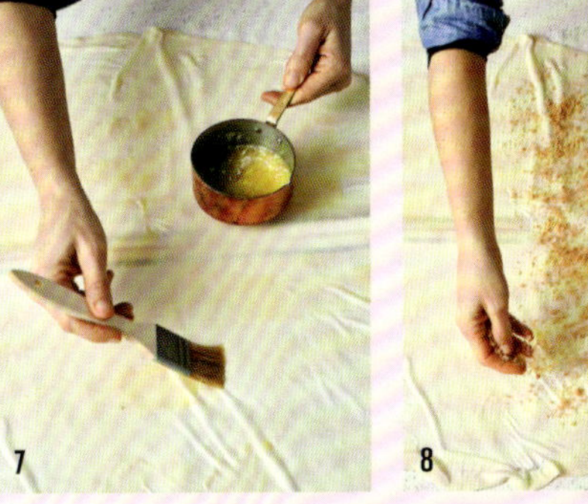

1. Shape the strudel dough into a ball, rub with a few drops of oil, and let rest.

2.+3. Roll out the strudel dough on the work surface until it is very thin.

4. Dust a large dish towel or tablecloth evenly with flour, then slide your hands flat under the dough.

5.+6. Stretch the dough over the backs of your hands working from the center outward, making the pastry thinner and thinner until you can see the cloth through it.

7. Brush the strudel dough with a thin layer of melted butter.

8. Depending on the recipe, sprinkle crumbs over the pastry, leaving a gap of about 2 in (5 cm) around the edge.

9. Spread the filling over the pastry.

10.+11. Fold in the edges of the pastry toward the center and use the cloth to help you loosely roll up the strudel from the short side.

12. Slide the strudel onto a baking sheet lined with parchment paper, so the seam is underneath when baked.

Apple Strudel

There is always something magical about stretching out the strudel dough so it is as thin as possible and almost transparent. And there is no doubt that this task is even more enjoyable if done in leisurely fashion in the company of friends or family, all gathered around the dough. The final result tastes even better with the addition of whipped cream or custard.

For 1 strudel

FOR THE STRUDEL DOUGH

200g type 00 flour, plus extra for working
pinch of salt
2 tbsp oil, plus more for rubbing in
110g lukewarm water

FOR THE FILLING

1.5–2kg acidic apples (e.g. Granny Smith, Braeburn, or Jonathan)
juice of 1 organic lemon and ½ tsp finely grated zest
60–70g superfine sugar, divided
50–60g raisins
splash of rum
120g butter
120g fine breadcrumbs
1 tsp ground cinnamon

TO SERVE

powdered sugar for dusting

FOR THE DOUGH Work the flour, salt, oil, and water together by hand until you have a smooth, stretchy dough. Shape into a ball and rub in a few drops of oil. Place in a bowl, cover with a plate, and let rest at room temperature for about 30 minutes.

FOR THE FILLING Meanwhile, peel, quarter, and core the apples. Slice the apples (not too thinly) and mix in a bowl with the juice and zest of the lemon, 30–40g of the superfine sugar (depending on how sweet the apples are), raisins, and rum. Melt 60g of butter in a pan and fry the breadcrumbs, stirring until light brown. Stir in the cinnamon and the remaining 30g of sugar.

Preheat the oven to 350°F (180°C). Line a baking sheet with parchment paper.

Dust a large dish towel or tablecloth evenly with flour. Roll out the strudel dough on this cloth as thinly as possible. Then slide your flat hands under the pastry and stretch it over the backs of your hands, working from the center outward, making the pastry thinner and thinner until you can see the cloth through it. Don't worry if there are little holes here and there.

Melt the remaining 60g of butter, let it cool down slightly, then lightly brush the strudel dough with 3 tablespoons of melted butter. Sprinkle the breadcrumbs over the pastry, leaving a gap of about 2 in (5 cm) around the edge. Create a strand of apple slices along the short side of the pastry.

→

Fold in the edges of the pastry toward the middle. Using the cloth, loosely roll up the strudel from the short side, and place it seam-side down on the lined baking sheet. Brush the strudel with the remaining melted butter and bake on the middle shelf of the oven for 35–40 minutes until golden.

Enjoy the strudel lukewarm or let it cool down. Dust with powdered sugar before serving.

Simmer the apple peel and cores with about 500g of naturally cloudy apple juice for 30–40 minutes to make a syrup. Use the apple syrup for glazes and cocktails or for sweetening oatmeal and salad dressings.

Quark Dumplings with Stewed Plums

This dough could not be any quicker to put together, and yet it is so light and fluffy these dumplings melt in the mouth. You can swap the stewed plums for any seasonal stewed fruit or compote. Instead of rolling the mixture into neat balls, you can also make the dumplings into other shapes, if preferred.

For 12 dumplings

FOR THE DUMPLINGS

250g full-fat quark or other curd cheese
40g semolina, plus extra for working
20g fine breadcrumbs
2 tbsp sunflower oil
1 egg
½ tsp organic lemon zest
pinch of salt, plus more for the cooking water
sugar for the cooking water

FOR THE CRUMBS

50g fine breadcrumbs
3 tbsp superfine sugar
½ tsp ground cinnamon
20g butter

TO SERVE

Stewed Plums (see p.212)
powdered sugar for dusting

FOR THE DUMPLINGS Use a wooden spoon to combine all the ingredients in a bowl, cover, and refrigerate for 15 minutes. Then shape the dough into twelve round dumplings and put them on a plate that has been sprinkled with semolina.

Fill a large saucepan with water, add ½ teaspoon each of salt and sugar, and bring to a boil. Lower the heat and gently slip the dumplings into the water. Cover and cook gently over very low heat for 15–20 minutes.

FOR THE CRUMBS Toast the breadcrumbs, sugar, cinnamon, and butter in a pan until golden.

Scoop the dumplings out of the water with a slotted spoon, drain briefly on paper towels, then roll in the crumbs. Arrange the dumplings on top of the Stewed Plums (which can be cold or slightly warm) and serve sprinkled with additional crumbs and powdered sugar.

Carnival Doughnuts

These sweet treats are fried in oil and are closely associated with carnival season in many parts of the world. The classic recipe features an apricot jam filling, but Diplomat Cream (see p.80) is another great option.

FOR THE DOUGH Melt the butter over low heat. Add the milk. Put the remaining ingredients except the oil in the bowl of a stand mixer, then add the butter and milk. Knead the dough on a low setting for 3 minutes (using the dough hook attachment). Cover with plastic wrap and let rest for 5 minutes, then knead again on a medium setting for 7 minutes. Shape into a ball, cover with plastic wrap, and let rise in a warm place for about 20 minutes.

Use a rolling pin to roll out the dough on a floured work surface until it is about ½ in (1 cm) thick, then stamp out 2¼–2¾-in (6–7-cm) circles. Cover the donuts and let rise on a floured surface for another 20 minutes.

FOR FRYING Heat the oil to 360°F (180°C) in a deep pot (check with a thermometer). Carefully place 3–4 donuts at a time in the hot oil, cover, and fry for about 3 minutes. Then turn and continue frying for another 3 minutes with the lid off. Remove the donuts with a slotted spoon and drain on paper towels.

FOR THE FILLING Put the jam in a piping bag fitted with a filling nozzle, and pipe it into the donuts. Dust with powdered sugar to serve.

Shape the remaining dough into little balls, let rise for 20 minutes, fry, and serve dusted with sugar.

For about 30 donuts

FOR THE YEAST DOUGH

100g butter
250g milk
30g fresh yeast (see p.110 for converting to dried)
50g superfine sugar
500g all-purpose flour, plus extra for the work surface
5 egg yolks
finely grated zest of ½ organic lemon
pinch of salt
1 tsp rum

FOR FRYING

2 liters oil

FOR THE FILLING

250g smooth apricot jam (see p.207–209)

TO SERVE

powdered sugar for dusting

KLEINES CAFÉ
CASH ONLY
CASH ONLY!
SPECTACLES

Austrian Sweet Buns

Once again, it doesn't matter whether you prefer these plain or with custard—they always taste delicious. Often these light and fluffy buns are also filled with apricot jam.

Makes about 20

FOR THE YEAST DOUGH

125g milk, divided
260g all-purpose flour, divided
40g superfine sugar
15g fresh yeast (see p.110 for converting to dried)
40g butter, plus extra for greasing
2 egg yolks
1 egg
1 tsp finely grated organic lemon zest
1 tsp rum
generous pinch of salt

FOR TOSSING

100g butter

TO SERVE

powdered sugar for dusting

FOR THE DOUGH Mix 100g of the milk, 30g of the flour, 1 teaspoon of the sugar, and the yeast to make a pre-dough. Cover with plastic wrap and let rise for about 20 minutes in a warm place.

Melt the butter and allow to cool slightly. Then put the pre-dough with the remaining ingredients in the bowl of a stand mixer and (using the dough hook attachment) knead for 3 minutes on a low setting. Cover with plastic wrap and let rest for 10 minutes. Next, knead the dough on a moderate setting for 7 minutes until it is smooth and coming away from the sides. Remove the dough from the bowl, shape it into a ball, and return it to the bowl. Cover and let rise for 1–1½ hours until roughly doubled in volume.

Preheat the oven to 350°F (180°C). Butter an 8-in (20-cm) round baking pan.

Divide the dough into pieces weighing about 30g and shape into balls.

FOR TOSSING Melt the butter and toss the dough balls so they are completely covered. Then place them snugly together in the pan seam-side down. Cover and let rise for another 1–1½ hours. Brush the little buns with the remaining butter (melted again if necessary). Bake on the middle shelf for 30–40 minutes. Serve dusted with plenty of powdered sugar.

Quark Turnovers

A creamy quark filling is wrapped in crisp, buttery pastry. These sweet palm-size parcels are best eaten with your fingers and are a fabulous outdoor snack.

For 9 turnovers

FOR THE ROUGH PUFF PASTRY

225g type 00 flour, plus extra for the work surface
1 tbsp superfine sugar
2g salt
150g cold butter
75g very cold water

FOR THE FILLING

50g butter, at room temperature
100g superfine sugar
2 egg yolks
250g full-fat quark or other curd cheese
2 tbsp cornstarch
seeds from ½ vanilla bean
2 tbsp raisins

FOR BRUSHING

1 egg
pinch of salt
2 tbsp whipping cream

TO SERVE

powdered sugar for dusting

FOR THE PASTRY Combine the flour, sugar, and salt and create a mound on the work surface. Dice the butter and roughly work it into the flour with a dough scraper, then crumble the mixture between your fingertips so some larger pieces of butter remain. Work in the water, press the pastry together (do not knead), wrap in plastic wrap and refrigerate for at least 1 hour.

Roll out the pastry on a floured work surface to about 6 × 12 in (15 × 30 cm). Fold it twice to create three layers, one on top of the other (like a letter). Turn the pastry 90 degrees, then roll it and fold it again as just described. Lightly press the layers with the rolling pin, wrap the pastry in plastic wrap, and refrigerate for at least 1 hour.

FOR THE FILLING Meanwhile, cream the butter and sugar until light and fluffy, then stir in the egg yolks, quark, cornstarch, and vanilla. Finally add the raisins.

Preheat the oven to 400°F (200°C). Line a baking sheet with parchment paper.

FOR BRUSHING Separate the egg. Mix the egg white with salt, and the yolk with cream. Remove the pastry from the fridge and roll it out on a floured work surface until it is about ⅛ in (3 mm) thick and about 12 in (30 cm) square. Using a fluted pastry wheel, slice the pastry into 4-in (10-cm) squares and place these on the lined baking sheet, ensuring there are sufficient gaps in between. Lightly brush with the egg white, then put 1 tablespoon of the filling in the middle of each square. Now fold the opposite sides of each square inward, gently pressing them together. Brush with the yolk and cream, spray liberally with water, and bake on the middle shelf of the oven for about 20 minutes until golden.

Remove the pastries from the oven, let cool briefly, and serve dusted with powdered sugar.

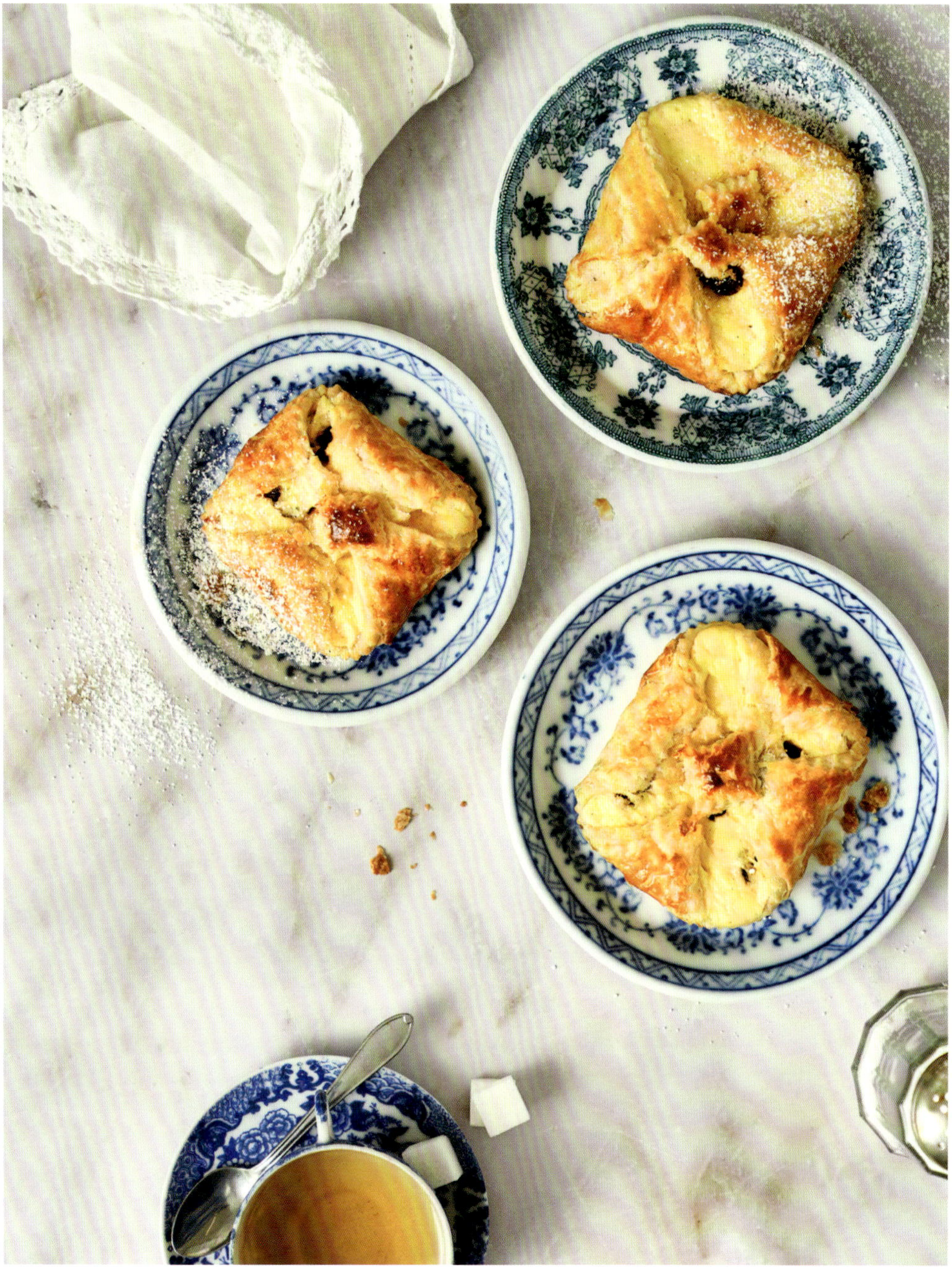

TIP

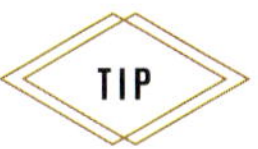

If you like, you can make the pastry squares slightly smaller and stamp out decorative shapes from the leftover pastry to add to the turnovers.

Apple Rings

Tart apples are dipped in batter with a touch of spice, then fried until golden. This ensures the apples have a creamy texture while still retaining a nice bite. In combination with the crisp batter and plenty of cinnamon sugar, the result is a perfect harmony of taste and texture.

Serves 4

FOR THE BATTER

3 eggs
200g type 00 flour
150g milk
½ tsp finely grated organic lemon zest
pinch of salt
pinch of ground cinnamon
100g sparkling mineral water
20g superfine sugar

FOR THE APPLE RINGS

4 large tart apples (e.g. Granny Smith, Braeburn, or Jonathan)
juice of 1 lemon

FOR FRYING

2 liters oil

FOR THE CINNAMON SUGAR

100g superfine sugar
1 tsp ground cinnamon

FOR THE BATTER Separate the eggs. Combine the flour, milk, egg yolks, lemon zest, salt, and cinnamon in a bowl, stirring everything together until smooth. Add the sparkling water and stir again until smooth. Whisk the egg whites and sugar in a scrupulously clean bowl until holding stiff peaks, then carefully fold into the flour mixture.

FOR THE RINGS Peel the apples and use an apple corer to remove the core. Slice the apples into rings about ½ in (1 cm) thick and drizzle with lemon juice. Alternatively, you can slice the apples immediately after peeling, then remove the core using a small round cutter.

FOR FRYING Pour oil into a deep pan to a depth of about 4 in (10 cm) and heat to 340°F (170°C), checking the temperature with a thermometer. Draw the apple rings through the batter one at a time using a fork, then slip them gently in batches into the hot oil. Fry for about 2 minutes on each side until golden. Lift the apple slices out of the oil with a slotted spoon and drain on paper towels. Repeat until all the apple rings have been cooked.

FOR THE CINNAMON SUGAR Combine the sugar and cinnamon. Dust the apple rings in the cinnamon sugar to serve.

Apricot Dumplings

When apricot season begins in Austria, it rains apricot dumplings all over the country. And these delicious treats—with their fluffy dough and a sweet cinnamon and butter crumb surrounding a tart apricot filling—are not just served for dessert. It is quite common to serve these dumplings as a "sweet main course" too. And needless to say, everyone makes the most of this custom.

For 14–16 dumplings

FOR THE DUMPLINGS

120g butter
500g full-fat quark or other curd cheese
pinch of finely grated organic lemon zest
4 egg yolks
300g type 00 flour, plus extra for the work surface
pinch of salt, plus more for the cooking water
sugar for the cooking water
14–16 apricots (depending on size), stones removed

TO SERVE

50g butter
powdered sugar for dusting

FOR THE CRUMBS

200g fine breadcrumbs
30g superfine sugar
1 tsp ground cinnamon
100g butter

FOR THE DUMPLINGS Melt the butter and allow to cool slightly. Stir the quark, lemon zest, and egg yolks together until smooth, then stir in the melted butter. Now add the flour and a pinch of salt and quickly work everything together to make a smooth dough. Let rest in the fridge for between 1 hour and 1 day.

Fill a large saucepan with water, add a pinch of salt and sugar, and bring to a boil.

Roll out the dough to create a strand on a floured work surface, cut as many pieces of dough as you have apricots, and shape each one into a ball. Flatten each ball so you can wrap it around an apricot and press the seam firmly to seal. Roll the dumplings so they are as round as possible and immediately slip them into the boiling water. Gently shake the pan a few times to prevent the dumplings from sticking to the bottom. Cover and cook over very low heat for 15–20 minutes.

BUTTER TO SERVE Meanwhile, melt the butter over moderate heat, stirring constantly until it is browning. This prevents the whey from settling, which would detract from the flavor. Once the butter starts to smell nutty, it is ready. Strain it through a fine mesh strainer and set aside.

FOR THE CRUMBS Toast the breadcrumbs, sugar, cinnamon, and butter in a pan until golden.

Scoop the dumplings out of the water with a slotted spoon, drain briefly on paper towels, and roll in the crumbs. Arrange the dumplings on plates with additional crumbs and powdered sugar, then drizzle with brown butter to serve.

Apricot Pancakes

The German name for this recipe Palatschinken *comes from the Slavic word* palačinka, *meaning "small pancakes." And these are a popular dish in many countries. In Vienna, people like to eat them with apricot jam and dusted with powdered sugar. This is another recipe that works wonderfully as an occasional "sweet main course," especially if you are feeding children, who tend to have a sweet tooth.*

Makes about 8

FOR THE PANCAKE BATTER

about 5 tbsp butter
200g milk
120g sparkling mineral water
200g type 00 flour
2 eggs
pinch of salt

TO ASSEMBLE

150g apricot jam (see p.207)
powdered sugar for dusting

FOR THE BATTER Melt the butter. Stir the milk, sparkling water, and flour together until smooth. Add the eggs and salt and stir again until smooth. Finally, stir in 3 tablespoons of melted butter.

Heat a shallow nonstick pan and grease with melted butter. Use a ladle to pour some batter into the center, then tilt the pan to spread it out in a thin, even layer. Fry the pancake over moderate heat for about 1 minute until golden brown, then turn and continue cooking for 30 seconds–1 minute. Cover and keep warm on a plate. Continue in the same way until you have used all the batter.

TO ASSEMBLE Spread the pancakes with apricot jam, roll them up, and arrange two pancakes on each plate. Dust with powdered sugar to serve.

Kaiserschmarren

Like many other legends, we will probably never know the true story of how Kaiserschmarren ("Emperor's shredded pancakes") got their name. Some say it was because Kaiser Franz Joseph I was served a similar rustic dish with particularly fine ingredients, others say the recipe was originally created for his wife, Elisabeth (Sisi), and that Kaiser Franz Joseph had them named after himself because he found them so delicious.

Serves 4

FOR THE PANCAKE BATTER

40g raisins
1 tsp rum
4 eggs, at room temperature
120g all-purpose flour
250g milk
1 tbsp vanilla sugar (see p.200)
pinch of salt
80g superfine sugar, divided
50g butter

TO SERVE

powdered sugar for dusting

FOR THE BATTER Soak the raisins in the rum, ideally overnight, or for at least 2 hours.

Preheat the oven to 400°F (200°C).

Separate the eggs. Use a balloon whisk to combine the flour, milk, vanilla sugar, and salt in a bowl until smooth. Then add the egg yolks and whisk again until smooth. Whisk the egg whites with 50g of the sugar in a scrupulously clean bowl until you have creamy stiff peaks, then gently fold into the batter.

Drain the raisins, and squeeze out some of the liquid if necessary. Heat the butter in a large, ovenproof pan or flat roasting dish, pour in the batter, and sprinkle with the rum-infused raisins. Bake on the lowest shelf of the oven for 8–10 minutes.

Use a spatula to split the pancakes into four, then turn each quarter over and continue cooking for about 3 minutes until done. Using two forks, tear the pancakes into uneven pieces, sprinkle with the remaining 30g of sugar, then caramelize in the oven or on the stove. Arrange the shredded pancakes on plates and dust with powdered sugar to serve.

Apple purée and/or Stewed Plums (see p.212) go wonderfully with these pancakes.

IOSEPHO II. AVGVSTO
ET
MARIA THERESIA AVGVSTA
IMPERANTIB.
ERECT. CIƆIƆCCLXXV.

Yeast Dumplings

This dish was a weekly fixture at the royal dining table during the reign of Empress Maria Theresa. Nowadays, these light and fluffy dumplings are standard fare at any Austrian ski hut. But this recipe proves that you can rustle up your own version of these dumplings very quickly, and they taste far better too.

Serves 4

FOR THE YEAST DOUGH

20g butter, plus extra for greasing
130g milk, plus extra for steaming
1 egg
250g all-purpose flour, plus extra for the work surface
15g fresh yeast (see p.110 for converting to dried)
pinch of salt
20g superfine sugar

FOR THE CUSTARD (OPTIONAL)

1 vanilla bean
300g milk
1 tsp rum
50g superfine sugar
1 tsp cornstarch
4 egg yolks

FOR THE FILLING

8 tsp plum butter (unsweetened plum spread)

TO SERVE

3 tbsp ground poppy seeds
3 tbsp powdered sugar
150g butter (as desired)

FOR THE DOUGH Melt the butter, then combine it with all the other ingredients in the bowl of a stand mixer and (using the dough hook attachment) knead for about 8 minutes until you have a very smooth dough. Cover with plastic wrap and let rise for about 1 hour in a warm place.

FOR THE CUSTARD Meanwhile, slice the vanilla bean in half lengthwise and scrape out the seeds with a small, sharp knife. In a saucepan, whisk together the vanilla bean and seeds, milk, rum, sugar, cornstarch, and egg yolks. Heat to just below the boiling point, stirring constantly, over moderate heat. As soon as the custard begins to thicken, remove from the heat and continue stirring for about 2 minutes. Strain it through a fine mesh strainer into a screw-top jar and seal.

Tip the dough out of the bowl. Divide it into four equal pieces, shape into balls on a floured work surface, cover with plastic wrap, and let prove for 15 minutes.

FOR THE FILLING Press the dough balls flat and put about 2 teaspoons of plum butter on each one. Carefully lift up the sides and squeeze them together to gently but securely seal each ball. Cover with plastic wrap and let rise for about 30 minutes.

In a saucepan with a steamer insert, add a splash of milk and just enough water to ensure that the insert isn't touching the liquid. Bring to a boil, lower the heat, and line the steamer with parchment paper and grease with butter. Steam the dumplings on the parchment paper for 20 minutes with the lid closed.

TO SERVE Mix the poppy seeds and powdered sugar. Melt the butter over moderate heat, stirring constantly until it is browning. Strain the brown butter through a fine mesh strainer.

Carefully lift the dumplings out of the steamer insert and allow any water to drip off. Arrange the dumplings on plates. Either pour the custard around the dumplings, or drizzle with brown butter. Sprinkle with poppy seeds and sugar to serve.

Immediately after lifting the dumplings out of the steamer, pierce each one several times with a thick needle or toothpick. This prevents them from collapsing.

Bohemian Pancakes

Known in German as Böhmische Dalken or Liwanzen. *This is a Bohemian dessert made using a yeast dough, which is a bit like a pancake. Traditionally, these are made in a special mini pancake pan, but a normal skillet works fine too. Often they are served sprinkled with poppy seeds, sugar, and cinnamon.*

Serves 6

FOR THE YEAST BATTER

125g milk, divided
10g fresh yeast (see p.110 for converting to dried)
20g superfine sugar
120g all-purpose flour, plus extra for the pan
20g butter, plus extra for the pan
1 egg
pinch of salt
1 tsp finely grated organic lemon zest

TO SERVE

125g sour cream
125g plum butter (unsweetened plum spread)
powdered sugar for dusting

FOR THE BATTER Heat half the milk until it is lukewarm, then add it to the yeast, 1 teaspoon of the sugar, and 2 tablespoons of the flour in a large bowl. Stir until smooth. Cover this pre-ferment with plastic wrap and let prove for about 15 minutes in a warm place.

Melt the butter over moderate heat, then let cool slightly. Separate the egg. Add the remaining flour and milk, the egg yolk, salt, lemon zest, and melted butter to the pre-ferment, and stir with a wooden spoon until smooth. Once again, cover and let prove for 30 minutes until little bubbles form on the surface.

If you are using a special mini pancake pan, grease the molds liberally with butter and dust with flour, and preheat the oven to 350°F (180°C). Alternatively, you can use a skillet.

Whisk the egg white with the remaining sugar in a scrupulously clean bowl until stiff, then fold into the yeast batter. Pour 2 tablespoons of batter into each greased pancake mold, and bake on the middle shelf of the oven for about 10 minutes until the surface is no longer shiny. Carefully turn the little pancakes with a fork and bake for about another 5 minutes until done.

Alternatively, you can cook these pancakes in a standard skillet: put 2 tablespoons of batter into the pan for each pancake, and cook on the stove until the surface is no longer shiny, then flip the pancakes over and continue cooking for about 1 minute until golden. Keep the cooked pancakes warm in a low oven.

TO SERVE Stir the sour cream until smooth. Put plum butter and sour cream on half the little pancakes and top each one with a second pancake. Dust with powdered sugar to serve.

Pastry Pillows

In German, these pastries are called Polsterzipf, *which means "pillow corner" due to their resemblance to a feather pillow. This is a classic Viennese delicacy, which has been immensely popular for centuries among fans of all things sweet. The origins of this recipe can be traced back to the 18th century, when it was first introduced to Austria's imperial court.*

For 25–30 pillows

FOR THE QUARK PASTRY

120g quark or other curd cheese

120g butter, very soft

2 egg yolks

500g type 00 flour, plus extra for the work surface

125g milk

generous pinch of salt

FOR FRYING

1 liter oil

TO SERVE

powdered sugar for dusting

FOR THE PASTRY Stir the quark and butter together in a bowl until smooth. Add the egg yolks and stir again until smooth. Now add the flour, milk, and salt, and quickly work everything together to make a smooth dough. Cover and let rest in the fridge for at least 1 hour.

FOR FRYING Heat the oil to 360°F (180°C) in a deep pot (check with a thermometer).

Roll out the pastry on a floured work surface until it is ⅛ in (3–4 mm) thick, then cut out triangles (pillows) in various sizes using a pastry wheel.

Fry the pastry triangles, in batches, in the oil until golden brown, turning once during cooking. Lift the pastry pillows out of the oil with a slotted spoon, drain on paper towels, and dust with powdered sugar to serve.

Christmas Baking

As the days grow shorter and ever frostier, as the first fires flicker in the hearth and the very first snowflakes dance from the sky, the craving for Lebkuchen (see p.176), Vanilla Crescents (see p.171), and traditional Austrian Spitzbuben (see p.192) grows ever stronger. That's because all these treats brighten our spirits with their warming spices, and they are also excellent for dunking in hot chocolate.

Cinnamon Stars

A Christmas classic that contains no flour at all. Nuts and meringue ensure a really moist consistency. And the irresistible aroma of cinnamon is something you can never tire of.

Makes about 30

FOR THE COOKIE DOUGH

90g egg whites at room temperature (from about 3 eggs)
250g powdered sugar
1 tsp lemon juice
3g ground cinnamon
350g ground almonds or hazelnuts, or a mixture of both, plus more for working

FOR THE COOKIE DOUGH Beat the egg whites, powdered sugar, and lemon juice in a scrupulously clean bowl until stiff. Weigh 130g of this meringue mixture for the glaze and set aside. Add the cinnamon and nuts to the remaining meringue mixture.

Preheat the oven to 275°F (140°C). Line a baking sheet with parchment paper.

Roll out the dough on a work surface sprinkled with ground almonds and/or hazelnuts to a thickness of ⅓ in (8 mm–1 cm). Spread the meringue mixture that you set aside earlier evenly over the dough with an angled palette knife. The best tool for stamping out the star shapes is a special cinnamon star cutter (these are designed with a hinge so they can be opened to remove the stars without damaging the meringue), but a standard cookie cutter will work too. Stamp out the star shapes as close together as possible. While you are working, occasionally dip the star cutter in hot water and dry it slightly to make it easier to remove the stars.

Use an angled palette knife to transfer the stars to the lined baking sheet, leaving at least a ¾-in (2-cm) gap in between, then bake on the middle shelf of the oven for about 15 minutes, checking them regularly. The white glaze should only go very slightly brown, and the stars should still be soft inside. The stars are ready as soon as they can be easily removed from the parchment paper. Let cool on the baking sheet.

For a faster version without stamping out star shapes, just slice the rolled out dough with its meringue glaze into strips or little bars. In Austria, we call these *Pariserstangerl* (Parisian bars).

Damenkapritzen

Damenkapritzen translates as "ladies' fancies." These fine pastries are trimmed with a light meringue, rather like a neatly ironed lace collar. Beneath this, there is a glimpse of an apricot-colored complexion. A cookie that keeps pace with the latest fashion.

Makes about 30

FOR THE COOKIE DOUGH

150g cold butter
300g type 00 flour, plus extra for the work surface
100g powdered sugar
seeds from ½ vanilla bean
½ tsp finely grated organic lemon zest
2 egg yolks
pinch of salt

FOR THE MERINGUE

60g egg whites at room temperature (from about 2 eggs)
pinch of salt
60g powdered sugar
20g superfine sugar

FOR BRUSHING

150g smooth apricot jam *(see p.207)*
1 tsp rum

FOR THE COOKIE DOUGH Cut the butter into cubes and use your fingertips to rub it into the flour, powdered sugar, and vanilla. Add the remaining ingredients and work everything swiftly together until you have a smooth dough. Wrap in plastic wrap and refrigerate for about 1 hour.

Preheat the oven to 350°F (180°C). Line a baking sheet with parchment paper.

Roll out the dough on a floured work surface until it is about ⅛ in (4 mm) thick, then stamp out 2-in (5-cm) circles. Combine any leftover dough and repeat the steps above. Place the circles about ¾ in (2 cm) apart on the lined baking sheet, then bake on the middle shelf of the oven for 8–10 minutes until light brown. Let cool on a wire rack.

FOR THE MERINGUE Meanwhile, use a hand mixer to beat the egg whites, salt, and both types of sugar in a scrupulously clean bowl over a pan of hot water until the sugar has dissolved completely. Continue whisking the mixture in a stand mixer (using the balloon whisk attachment) for 20 minutes until it reaches meringue consistency. Transfer to a piping bag fitted with a ¼-in (5-mm) star nozzle.

Lower the oven temperature to 300°F (150°C).

FOR BRUSHING Heat the jam with the rum. Brush the top of the cookies with jam, pipe meringue around the edge, and bake on the middle shelf of the oven for 8–10 minutes. Let cool on a wire rack.

Vanilla Crescents

The Queen of Christmas baking: the Vanilla Crescent. They have nostalgic associations, evoking the Advent season and a sense of warmth, and their origins can be traced back to the 17th century. Often the little crescents are tossed in vanilla sugar while still warm. I like to dust them with powdered sugar as if they have been coated in freshly fallen snow.

Makes 40–50 cookies

FOR THE COOKIE DOUGH

220g cold butter
280g type 00 flour
70g powdered sugar
50g ground almonds
50g ground hazelnuts
1 tsp finely grated organic lemon zest

FOR THE VANILLA SUGAR

150g powdered sugar
seeds from ½ vanilla bean

FOR THE COOKIE DOUGH Cut the butter into cubes and use your fingertips to rub it into the flour, powdered sugar, ground almonds and hazelnuts, and the lemon zest. Quickly work everything together to make a smooth dough, press slightly flat, wrap in plastic wrap, and rest in the fridge for at least 2 hours or overnight.

Preheat the oven to 350°F (180°C). Line a baking sheet with parchment paper.

Shape about one-third of the chilled dough into rolls that are as thick as a finger, then slice into pieces about 1¼ in (3 cm) long. Mold these pieces into crescents, and place them on the lined baking sheet, ensuring there are sufficient gaps in between. Bake on the middle shelf of the oven for 10–12 minutes until golden. Continue in the same way until you have used all the dough.

FOR THE VANILLA SUGAR Mix the powdered sugar with the vanilla, then sift onto the baked cookies while they are still warm. Alternatively, toss the crescents carefully in the sifted powdered sugar.

How to make ...

Shortcrust pastry

Shortcrust pastry has a firm texture and is usually made without any raising agents. The word "short" refers to the soft and delicate texture. A particularly crisp texture can be achieved by incorporating butter into the dough so tiny pieces are still visible. .

The **main ingredients** in shortcrust are usually

Fat: butter, lard, or margarine

Flour: all-purpose flour, spelt flour, whole wheat flour, or other types of flour

Sugar: superfine sugar, powdered sugar, or brown sugar

Eggs/water: whole egg, egg yolks, or water

A classic ratio for the ingredients in shortcrust is 3:2:1

3 parts flour,
2 parts butter,
1 part sugar

The essentials

CHILL THE INGREDIENTS

The butter, flour, and egg should be kept cold to ensure a lovely short texture.

WORK THE PASTRY QUICKLY

The ingredients should be worked quickly. If you handle the pastry for too long, it will become tough and brittle. In this scenario we describe the pastry as having been "overworked."

REST THE PASTRY

Shape the pastry into a ball, wrap it in plastic wrap, and let it rest in the fridge for at least 30 minutes.

Variations

You can add a variety of different flavors: for example, vanilla, lemon zest, orange zest, cocoa powder, or spices such as cinnamon or cardamom.

- If the pastry is too dry, add cold water or milk 1 TB at a time. If the pastry becomes too tough or brittle, it helps to add some egg whites.
- If any pastry is left over, you can store it in the fridge for a few days or even freeze it.

1. Put diced cold butter in a bowl with flour and sugar.

2. Rub the ingredients together between fingertips.

3. Add the egg.

4. Quickly work everything together.

5. Knead once.

6. Shape the pastry into a ball.

7. Roll out the pastry and place it in the pan using a rolling pin.

8. Press the pastry into the pan.

9. Trim the edge with a small knife.

Angel's Cheeks

These cookies are called "angel's cheeks" for obvious reasons, but this very versatile recipe can be made with whatever jam you prefer, and they are one of the most popular cookies in my family.

Makes about 30

FOR THE COOKIE DOUGH

220g cold butter
250g all-purpose flour, plus extra for dusting
150g ground blanched almonds
1 tsp baking powder
120g powdered sugar
pinch of salt
½ tsp aniseed
1 egg yolk

FOR THE FILLING

150g red currant jam (see p.208)

FOR THE COOKIE DOUGH Cut the butter into cubes. Use your fingertips to rub it into the flour, ground almonds, baking powder, powdered sugar, and salt in a bowl. Crush the aniseed using a pestle and mortar, add this to the bowl along with the egg yolk, and work everything together quickly to create a smooth dough. Wrap in plastic wrap and refrigerate for 2–3 hours.

Preheat the oven to 350°F (180°C). Line a baking sheet with parchment paper. If you have a wooden baking mold, dust it with flour.

Create marble-size balls out of the dough and press them into the wooden mold, if using. Remove the little cookies from the mold and place them about 1¼ in (3 cm) apart, with the motif facing up, on the lined baking sheet. Alternatively, if you don't have a mold, place the little balls of dough on the baking sheet with gaps of about 1¼ in (3 cm) in between, and create an indentation in each one using the handle of a wooden spoon. Bake on the middle shelf of the oven for 9–10 minutes until pale in color, then let cool on the baking sheet.

FOR THE FILLING Heat the jam slightly and use a small spoon to scoop it into the little dips in the cookies. Let cool.

Lebkuchen

Lebkuchen signify the start of the Advent season. With their enticing scent, they conjure up a feel-good festive spirit. They work beautifully in all sorts of different recipes: from gingerbread houses to Christmas tree decorations, and they can be filled with dried fruit or covered in chocolate or icing. Don't be put off by this recipe if candied fruit is not your thing—the candied lemon and orange are chopped very finely and, in combination with the nuts, ensure a wonderfully moist texture.

Makes 10–15

FOR THE DOUGH

250g honey
200g turbinado sugar
100g butter
30g candied lemon or orange peel
250g type 00 flour, plus extra for the work surface
250g rye flour
80g ground almonds or hazelnuts
½ tsp finely grated zest of an organic lemon or orange
2 tsp lebkuchen spice mix (available online or use mixed spice)
8g baking soda
1 tbsp milk
2 eggs

FOR BRUSHING

100g powdered sugar
20g lemon juice

FOR THE DOUGH Heat the honey, turbinado sugar, and butter over low heat until the sugar has dissolved, taking care to ensure the mixture never boils. Finely chop the candied lemon or orange peel in a food processor.

Mix both types of flour with the ground nuts, candied lemon or orange, lemon zest, and lebkuchen spice in the mixing bowl of a stand mixer. Dissolve the baking soda in the milk and add this to the flour mixture. Add the warm honey mixture and the eggs, then work everything quickly together to create the dough. Wrap the dough in plastic wrap and let rest in the fridge at least overnight and for up to 1 week.

Preheat the oven to 350°F (180°C). Line a baking sheet with parchment paper.

Roll out the dough on a floured work surface until it is ⅛ in (3–4 mm) thick, then press it into your chosen wooden molds (if using), or stamp out different shapes. Combine any leftover scraps of dough and repeat in the same way. Place the cookies on the lined baking sheet, leaving space in between, and bake on the middle shelf of the oven for 9–13 minutes, depending on the size. Let cool completely on a wire rack.

FOR BRUSHING Stir the powdered sugar and lemon juice until smooth and brush over the cookies.

A lovely variation is to brush the lebkuchen with egg before baking and press almonds, other nuts, or candied cherries into the dough.

Fruit Bread

Dried winter fruits, nuts, and warming spices combine in this majestic, sweet bread, which tastes fabulous spread with cold butter and sprinkled with salt, served alongside a cup of tea or coffee. It is also a wonderful fruity accompaniment for a cheese board.

FOR THE FRUIT MIXTURE If the figs and dried pears still have stalks, remove them, then chop both coarsely with the prunes and dates. Transfer the dried fruit to a large bowl, combine with the remaining ingredients, cover, and leave the flavors to infuse for at least 3 hours or overnight.

FOR THE DOUGH Heat the milk until lukewarm, add it to the flour, yeast, and turbinado sugar in the bowl of a stand mixer and (using the dough hook attachment) knead for 8 minutes. Cover the dough with plastic wrap and let rise for about 30 minutes in a warm place.

Add the soaked dried fruit and the soaking liquid to the dough, then knead well for 5 minutes. Put the dough into a panettone pan (or a cake or loaf pan that has been lined with parchment paper). Press the surface slightly flat with wet hands, cover, and let rise for about 2 hours.

Preheat the oven to 350°F (170°C).

FOR THE TOPPING Spread cherries and almonds over the surface of the cake and bake on the middle shelf of the oven for about 15 minutes. Lower the heat to 325°F (160°C) and bake for about 1 hour until done.

Remove the cake from the oven and let cool. Once cool, wrap in plastic wrap and allow to mature for 2 days. This cake will keep for about 1 month.

Makes 1 cake

FOR THE FRUIT MIXTURE

250g dried figs
250g dried pears
250g pitted prunes
50g pitted dried dates
200g raisins
100g hazelnuts
100g almonds
1 tsp lebkuchen spice mix
½ tsp salt
50g candied orange peel
20g honey
juice and finely grated zest of 1 organic orange
125g hot water
100g freshly brewed black tea or hot water

FOR THE YEAST DOUGH

150g milk
300g all-purpose flour
10g fresh yeast (see p.110 for converting to dried)
100g turbinado sugar

FOR THE TOPPING

candied cherries
blanched almonds

Stollen

The full array of Christmas aromas come together here, gently enveloped in a buttery yeast dough. Melted butter and powdered sugar cover the Stollen like a warm blanket, ensuring it stays fresh for weeks for optimal enjoyment.

Makes 1 stollen

FOR THE FRUIT MIXTURE

50g candied lemon peel
50g candied orange peel
200g raisins
40g rum

FOR THE DOUGH STARTER

15g fresh yeast (see p.110 for converting to dried)
90g milk
160g all-purpose flour
10g superfine sugar

FOR THE MAIN DOUGH

140g all-purpose flour, plus extra for working
½ tsp salt
10g milk
150g butter, at room temperature, plus extra for greasing

FOR THE FRUIT MIXTURE Chop the candied lemon and orange peel very finely. Mix with the raisins and rum and let the flavors infuse overnight.

FOR THE DOUGH STARTER The following day, put the yeast, milk, flour, and sugar into the bowl of a stand mixer and (using the dough hook attachment) knead for about 8 minutes until the dough is coming away from the sides of the bowl. Cover the dough with plastic wrap and let rise for 1–1½ hours in a warm place.

FOR THE MAIN DOUGH Knead all the ingredients in the bowl of a stand mixer. Add the starter, then knead both doughs together thoroughly.

FOR THE STOLLEN FLAVOR Add the ingredients for the stollen flavor to the dough and knead well. Slowly work in the fruit mixture. Shape the dough into a ball, cover, and let rise for about 30 minutes.

FOR THE FILLING Shape the marzipan into a log about 10 in (25 cm) long. Press the dough flat on a floured surface to about 4 × 10 in (10 × 25 cm), then place the marzipan in the middle of the dough and fold the dough over it. Make sure the seam is tightly sealed.

Brush a 10-in (25-cm) stollen pan with butter and dust with flour, then place the dough in it with the seam facing up. Cover and let rise for about 30 minutes.

FOR THE STOLLEN FLAVOR

50g sliced almonds
50g ground blanched almonds
35g superfine sugar
1 drop almond extract
6 cardamom pods, seeds removed and finely ground
¼ tsp aniseed, finely ground
½ tsp ground cinnamon
pinch of ground nutmeg
pinch of ground allspice
finely grated zest of ½ organic orange

FOR THE FILLING

100g marzipan

TO FINISH

100g butter, divided
50g superfine sugar
100g powdered sugar

→

Preheat the oven to 425°F (220°C).

Slide the stollen onto the middle shelf of the oven and lower the heat to 350°F (170°C). Bake for 50 minutes–1 hour, then let cool in the pan for about 20 minutes. Turn the stollen out of the pan and let cool for another 20 minutes.

TO FINISH Melt 50g of the butter and spread this over the stollen. Leave uncovered for about 12 hours somewhere that is not too warm to allow the flavors to develop. Then melt the remaining 50g of butter and brush this over the stollen. Sprinkle with the superfine sugar and leave uncovered to mature for another 12 hours, again selecting a location that is not too warm. (The butter and sugar form a layer that preserves the stollen.) Dust the stollen liberally with powdered sugar, wrap in plastic wrap, and let mature for 1–3 weeks at 54–61°F (12–16°C). This allows the stollen to develop its full flavor, and it will keep for at least 3 months.

CEC

Chocolate Kisses

The standard greeting in Vienna is a kiss on the left cheek and a kiss on the right—and this recipe gets its name from the German for kiss, "Bussi" *or* "Busserl." *When people are saying goodbye, they often just say* "Bussi, Baba" *(kisses and bye). These gestures are so heartfelt, Vienna's reputation for being rather grumpy is instantly forgotten. And these little Chocolate Kisses have a similar, if not even more magical, effect.*

Makes about 25

FOR THE MERINGUE MIX

60g egg whites at room temperature (from about 2 eggs)
pinch of salt
60g superfine sugar
60g powdered sugar
30g dark chocolate
1 tsp cornstarch
1 tsp cocoa powder
60g ground hazelnuts
¼ tsp ground cinnamon
1 tsp finely grated organic lemon zest

TO ASSEMBLE

about 25 edible wafer paper disks, about 2 in (5 cm) diameter
12–13 whole hazelnuts
70g dark chocolate

FOR THE MERINGUE MIX Use a hand mixer to beat the egg whites, salt, and both sugars in a scrupulously clean bowl over a pan of hot water until the sugar has dissolved completely. Continue whisking the mixture in a stand mixer (using the balloon whisk attachment) for 20 minutes until it reaches meringue consistency.

Preheat the oven to 275°F (140°C). Line a baking sheet with parchment paper.

Roughly chop the chocolate and melt it in a metal bowl over a pan of hot water. Sift the cornstarch and cocoa powder into a bowl and mix in the ground hazelnuts and cinnamon. Add the melted chocolate, hazelnut mixture, and lemon zest to the meringue and fold everything in. Transfer the mixture to a piping bag fitted with a smooth round nozzle.

TO ASSEMBLE Place the edible wafer paper disks about ¾ in (2 cm) apart on the lined baking sheet. Pipe the meringue mixture onto the edible wafer paper discs. Cut the hazelnuts in half with a sharp knife and press one into the center of each chocolate kiss. Bake on the middle shelf of the oven for about 12 minutes until they can easily be removed from the parchment paper. Let cool completely.

Roughly chop the chocolate, melt it in a metal bowl over a pan of hot water, and dip the base of each chocolate kiss in the chocolate. Place the kisses on parchment paper and let dry.

Florentines

An exquisite caramelized treat, which tastes of Christmas and even wins over people who don't like candied fruit.

Makes about 30

FOR THE CARAMELIZED ALMONDS

50g unsalted pistachios
30g candied cherries
30g candied orange peel
250g sliced almonds
50g type 00 flour
60g whipping cream
70g butter
pinch of salt
40g honey
60g superfine sugar

TO DECORATE

100–150g dark chocolate

Line a 8 × 12 in (20 × 30 cm) baking sheet or baking dish with parchment paper. Preheat the oven to 375°F (190°C).

FOR THE CARAMELIZED ALMONDS Chop the pistachios, candied cherries, and candied orange peel, but not too finely. Combine the sliced almonds and flour in a bowl.

Bring the cream, butter, salt, honey, and sugar to a boil in a pan and simmer over moderate heat for about 5 minutes. Lower the heat and stir in the almond and flour mixture, pistachios, and candied fruit.

Spread the mixture into the baking sheet or dish and bake on the middle shelf of the oven for about 12 minutes. Stamp out the Florentines with a round cutter while still lukewarm.

TO DECORATE Roughly chop the chocolate and melt it in a metal bowl over a pan of hot water. Dip the base of each Florentine into the chocolate to coat. Let set on a wire rack or sheet of parchment paper.

I usually nibble any leftovers straight from the baking sheet. But you can also roughly chop up any unused bits and add them to the Fruit Bread (see p.181), or chop them more finely and fold them into the Chocolate Kisses mixture (see p.186), or sprinkle them over your granola as a Christmas treat.

Ischler Cookies

Each cookie looks like an elegant little cake on the cookie platter. Luckily you can eat several of these in one sitting.

Makes about 20

FOR THE VANILLA CUSTARD

125g milk
10g cornstarch
seeds from 1 vanilla bean
1 egg yolk
25g superfine sugar

FOR THE COOKIE DOUGH

125g cold butter
250g type 00 flour, plus extra for the work surface
60g powdered sugar
½ tsp finely grated organic lemon zest
1 egg
pinch of salt

FOR THE PARISIAN CREAM

200g whipping cream
50g butter
1 tsp rum
200g dark chocolate (at least 65 percent cocoa)

TO ASSEMBLE

150g smooth apricot jam *(see p.207)*
150g dark chocolate
20g coconut oil
handful of pistachios

FOR THE VANILLA CUSTARD Combine 2 tablespoons of the milk with the cornstarch, vanilla, and egg yolk, and stir until smooth. Briefly bring the remaining milk and the sugar to a boil, then add the milk and cornstarch paste, stirring constantly. Continue stirring over low heat for 3 minutes until ready. Transfer into a bowl, cover with plastic wrap (the plastic and custard should be touching to prevent a skin from forming). Chill overnight.

FOR THE COOKIE DOUGH Cut the butter into cubes. Use your fingertips to rub the butter into the flour and powdered sugar. Add the remaining ingredients and work together to a smooth dough. Wrap in plastic wrap and chill for 1 hour or overnight.

FOR THE PARISIAN CREAM Heat the whipping cream, butter, and rum but do not allow to boil. Chop the chocolate into little pieces and dissolve in the hot cream mixture, stirring with a balloon whisk until smooth. Refrigerate for at least 2 hours.

Preheat the oven to 350°F (170°C). Line two baking sheets with parchment paper.

Roll out the dough on a floured work surface until it is 1 in (2.5 cm) thick, then stamp out 2-in (5-cm) circles. Combine the leftover cookie dough and repeat the steps above to create more shapes. Place the circles on one of the lined baking sheets, spacing them out sufficiently. Bake on the middle shelf of the oven for 10–12 minutes until golden. Let cool on a wire rack.

Whisk the Parisian cream for 3–4 minutes until it is like whipped cream. Pass the vanilla custard through a fine mesh strainer or process using an immersion blender. Combine with the Parisian cream and transfer this mixture into a piping bag fitted with a smooth round nozzle. Pipe onto half of the baked cookie circles and place a second cookie on top. Let set in the fridge.

TO ASSEMBLE Heat the jam and spread thinly over the cookies. Roughly chop the chocolate, melt in a metal bowl above a pan of hot water along with the coconut oil, and dip the little cookies in this mixture. Place on the second lined baking sheet to dry. Roughly chop the pistachios and use these to decorate.

Spitzbuben

A festive cookie jar classic, which is so simple, yet simply delicious. You can also experiment with all sorts of different cookie cutter shapes here, depending on what appeals. So these double-decker cookies can easily be adapted for any season.

For 30–40 cookies

FOR THE COOKIE DOUGH

150g cold butter

300g type 00 flour, plus extra for the work surface

100g powdered sugar, plus extra for dusting

seeds from ½ vanilla bean

½ tsp finely grated organic lemon zest

1 egg yolk

1 egg

pinch of salt

FOR THE FILLING

150g red currant jam (see p.208)

1 tsp rum

FOR THE COOKIE DOUGH Cut the butter into cubes. Use your fingertips to rub the butter into the flour and powdered sugar. Add the remaining ingredients and work everything swiftly together until you have a smooth dough. Wrap in plastic wrap and refrigerate for about 1 hour.

Preheat the oven to 350°F (180°C). Line a baking sheet with parchment paper.

Roll out the dough on a floured work surface until it is about 1 in (2.5 cm) thick, then stamp out 2-in (5-cm) circles. Create little cut-out shapes in half of these circles. Combine the leftover cookie dough and repeat the steps above to create more shapes. Place the circles on the lined baking sheet, making sure they are spaced out sufficiently, then bake on the middle shelf of the oven for 8–10 minutes until golden. Let cool on a wire rack.

FOR THE FILLING Heat the jam and rum. Spread the jam over the bottom of the cookie bases (without cut-outs). Dust the cookies with the holes with powdered sugar and place them on the jam-covered bases.

BIEN DES CHASSEURS SE VANTENT DU GIBIER QU'ILS NE TUENT PAS.
LUI AU CONTRAIRE EN TUE BEAUCOUP ET NE S'EN VANTE PAS

Puddings & Preserves

With every spoonful of Vanilla Custard with Whipped Cream (see p.200), a sensation washes over you that is simultaneously cozy, creamy, and cool, and you are instantly transported back to childhood memories.

Diplomat Pudding

For a long time this dessert was associated with the upper classes and was often served in fine private salons (Kabinetten), *so in German it is also known as* kabinettpudding. *In those days, the dish consisted of luxurious ingredients such as sponge, candied fruits, and liqueur. Over time, the recipe has evolved and has gradually been simplified so it is now more down to earth. Stale bread, rolls, or leftover cake and cookies can now be used as the basic ingredient.*

Serves 8–10

250g milk, divided
250g whipping cream, divided
80g superfine sugar, divided
seeds from 1 vanilla bean
pinch of salt
4 egg yolks
20g cornstarch
4 sheets of gelatin
150g soft prunes
25g Amarena cherries
100g sponge fingers or plain cookies

In a saucepan, slowly heat 200g of the milk, 125g of the whipping cream, 70g of the superfine sugar, the vanilla, and the salt.

In a separate bowl, mix the remaining 50g of milk and 10g of superfine sugar with the egg yolks and cornstarch. Add 2 tablespoons of the heated milk and cream mixture to level out the temperatures and dissolve any lumps of cornstarch. Add this mixture back to the saucepan and simmer over moderate heat for 2–3 minutes, stirring constantly, until it is creamy and has a lovely glossy sheen. Remove from the heat.

Soak the gelatin in cold water for about 5 minutes, squeeze it out thoroughly, and dissolve it in the warm milk mixture. Cover with plastic wrap and let cool slightly (the plastic should be in contact with the surface of the custard mixture to prevent a skin from forming). Then pass the cooled mixture through a fine mesh strainer or process with an immersion blender. Whisk the remaining 125g of whipping cream until stiff and fold into the dessert.

Rinse a 9½-in (24-cm) pudding mold with cold water and pour in half the mixture. Top with the prunes and cherries (keeping a couple back as decoration in each case), and sponge fingers or cookies, then add the remaining custard mixture. Cover and let set in the fridge for at least 6 hours, but ideally overnight.

Turn the dessert over to release it from the mold (you may need to run a small, sharp knife around the edge first to make it easier to turn the dessert out). Decorate the custard with the remaining prunes and cherries, and drizzle with cherry juice from the jar to serve.

Semolina Pudding

The German name for this pudding, flammeri, *is actually derived from the English "flummery" and refers to a cream that has been thickened using starch. Instead of stewed plums, a fruit compote or coulis also works well with this pudding.*

Serves 4

½ vanilla bean
1 cinnamon stick
120g superfine sugar
500g milk
1 organic orange
90g semolina
4 sheets of gelatin
500g whipping cream
150g Stewed Plums (see p.212)

Slice the vanilla bean in half lengthwise and scrape out the seeds with a small, sharp knife. Put the pod, seeds, cinnamon stick, sugar, and milk into a saucepan. Finely grate 1 tsp orange zest into the pan. Slowly heat the milk, but do not boil. Stir well to dissolve the sugar. Remove from the heat and let the flavors infuse for at least 20 minutes.

Strain the infused milk through a fine mesh strainer and return the liquid to the pan. Gradually add the semolina and bring to a boil, stirring constantly. Remove the pan from the heat, cover, and let stand for about 15 minutes. Soak the gelatin in cold water for about 5 minutes.

Squeeze the gelatin well and dissolve it in the still-warm semolina mixture. Squeeze the juice of the orange and stir this in too. Let cool.

Whisk the whipping cream until soft and creamy, then fold it, one spoonful at a time, into the semolina mixture, keeping back 4 tablespoons of cream for decoration.

Divide the semolina pudding among little dishes or glasses, cover with plastic wrap, and leave to set in the fridge (the plastic should be touching the surface of the pudding to prevent a skin from forming). Serve with Stewed Plums and the remaining whipped cream.

Vanilla Custard with Whipped Cream

This pudding is steeped in vivid childhood memories, which means it is a charmingly romantic option, too.

Serves 4

250g milk, divided
350g whipping cream, divided
40g superfine sugar, divided
seeds from 1 vanilla bean
pinch of salt
2 egg yolks
40g cornstarch
1 tsp powdered sugar

In a saucepan, slowly heat 170g of the milk, 250g of the whipping cream, 25g of the sugar, the vanilla and the salt.

In a separate bowl, mix the remaining 80g of milk and 15g of sugar with the egg yolks and cornstarch. Now add 2 tablespoons of the heated milk and cream mixture to level out the temperatures and dissolve any lumps of cornstarch. Add this mixture back to the saucepan and simmer over moderate heat for 2–3 minutes, stirring constantly, until it is creamy and has a lovely glossy sheen.

Rinse four 3¾-in (9-cm) pudding molds with cold water and immediately pour in the custard mixture. Cover and let set in the fridge for at least 2 hours or overnight.

Turn the little custards over to release them from the molds. You may need to run a small, sharp knife around the edge first to make it easier to turn the puddings out. Whisk the remaining 100g of whipping cream with the powdered sugar until thick. Serve the puddings with the whipped cream.

The scraped-out vanilla bean offers an easy way to make your own vanilla sugar. Just allow the bean to air dry, then chop it with 120g of powdered sugar using a food processor. Transfer to a screw-top jar and store in a dry location.

Reis à la Trauttmansdorff

This exquisite dessert is named after the aristocrat Ferdinand von Trauttmansdorff, who is said to have been particularly fond of sweet rice puddings and so became a kind of godfather for this dish.

Serves 4

80g short grain rice
250g milk
40g superfine sugar
½ vanilla bean
pinch of salt
1 tsp finely grated organic lemon zest
1 tsp finely grated organic orange zest
4 sheets of gelatin
250g whipping cream
handful of mixed berries
3 blood oranges
butter for the mold

Soak the rice in cold water for about 10 minutes. Line the bottom of a deep 5¼-in (13-cm) springform pan with parchment paper, and grease the sides with butter.

Heat the milk, sugar, vanilla bean, and salt in a saucepan and simmer until the sugar has dissolved. Rinse the rice under cold water in a fine mesh strainer and add it to the milk along with the lemon and orange zest. Cover and cook the rice over low heat for 15–20 minutes until soft. Remove from the heat and discard the vanilla bean.

Soak the gelatin in cold water for about 5 minutes. Squeeze it out well then dissolve it in the hot milk and rice. Transfer the rice to a bowl, cover, and let cool for 30–40 minutes.

Whisk the whipping cream until stiff. Depending on the size of the berries, cut them into smaller pieces or leave them whole, then carefully fold them into the cooled but not yet thickened rice along with the whipped cream. Pour the rice pudding mixture into the pan. Smooth the surface and let set in the fridge for at least 4 hours but ideally overnight.

Release the springform pan, remove the parchment paper, and put the rice pudding on a plate.

Use a small, sharp knife to completely cut away the skin of the blood oranges, then slice thinly. Decorate the rice pudding with sliced oranges and (if available) the orange leaves.

Jellied Oranges

A delightful jelly dessert, served in the hollowed-out orange skin to take the flavor to the next level. This never fails to grab attention at a festive meal.

Serves 4

6 organic oranges
3 sheets of gelatin
100g whipping cream (optional)

Cut the oranges in half and squeeze the juice. Scoop the remaining pulp out of four orange halves using a spoon. To make the orange halves stand better, cut off a very thin slice from the base of each one, making sure it is still intact so no liquid can escape later. Ideally place the orange halves in a muffin pan or four small bowls.

Soak the gelatin in cold water for about 5 minutes. Strain the orange juice through a fine mesh strainer and measure 250g of juice. Heat the juice in a small saucepan. Squeeze the gelatin well and dissolve it in the warm orange juice. Pour the liquid into the prepared orange halves. Transfer to the fridge and let set for at least 4 hours or overnight.

If desired, serve the orange jellies with freshly whipped cream or just enjoy them as they are.

By preserving the fruit at its ripest, we can evoke the spirit of summer all year round. And this jam is not just a blissful breakfast option, it also makes a wonderful filling for all sorts of cakes, cream slices, and roulades. You might like to experiment by replacing the apricots in the recipe below with other fruit—this is a quick and easy way to rustle up a whole range of different jams. For a really unique touch, try adding different flavors such as vanilla, cinnamon, lavender, ginger, or pepper.

Apricot Jam

Makes 6 (9fl oz/250ml) jars

about 1.2kg ripe apricots (1kg pitted weight)
about 500g jam sugar (2:1)
juice of 1 organic lemon
pinch of salt

Wash and halve the apricots. Remove the stones and slice into wedges. Weigh the fruit and combine with the appropriate quantity of jam sugar (half the weight of the fruit) in a pan. Let the flavors infuse for about 2 hours. This draws water out of the fruit, softens the pieces of fruit, and partially dissolves the sugar.

Heat this mixture together with the lemon juice and salt and let it simmer for 5–7 minutes, stirring constantly. If desired, use an immersion blender to finely purée the jam or you can just leave it as it is. If any foam has formed, let the jam stand for about 5 minutes before decanting it into jars. This allows the bubbles to rise to the surface, and the foam can then easily be scooped off with a spoon. Don't throw this away! Spread it on some buttered bread to test the flavor. Next check that your jam has set (see p.209).

Pour the jam into sterilized jars while it is still hot, leaving ½ in of space at the top of the jar. Wipe the rim, seal with a canning lid, and process in boiling water for 10 minutes. Let the jam cool and check to ensure all of the lids sealed properly.

Raspberry Jam

Makes 3 (9fl oz/250ml) jars

250g granulated sugar
4g pectin
500g raspberries
juice of 1 organic lemon

Combine the sugar, pectin, and raspberries in a pan and bring to a boil, stirring constantly. As soon as it starts to boil, add the lemon juice and cook at a rapid boil for about 5 minutes. Check to see whether the jam has reached setting point (see right).

Pour the jam into sterilized jars while it is still hot, leaving ½ in of space at the top of the jar. Wipe the rim, seal with a canning lid, and process in boiling water for 10 minutes. Let the jam cool and check to ensure all of the lids sealed properly.

The granulated sugar and pectin can be replaced by 250g jam sugar (2:1).

Redcurrant Jam

Makes 6 (9fl oz/250ml) jars

1kg red currants
500g jam sugar (2:1)

Bring the red currants to a boil, stirring constantly. Then press the cooked fruit through a fine mesh strainer or use a food mill.

Combine the red currant purée with the jam sugar, bring to a boil, and bubble vigorously for 4–6 minutes, stirring constantly. Check to see whether the jam has reached setting point (see right).

Pour the jam into sterilized jars while it is still hot, leaving ½ in of space at the top of the jar. Wipe the rim, seal with a canning lid, and process in boiling water for 10 minutes. Let the jam cool and check to ensure all of the lids sealed properly.

A shot of gin stirred into the jam before you decant it into jars helps bring out the flavor of the red currants.

Smooth Jam

To make jam with a smooth texture, pass the hot cooked fruit through a fine mesh strainer or use a food mill, and collect the puréed fruit in a bowl. Use a spatula to scrape the mixture back into the pan, cook for about 1 minute, then proceed as described. This process is a bit more time-consuming, but it creates a silky smooth jam.

TESTING THE SETTING POINT

Before making the jam, put a small saucer in the freezer. After cooking, put a couple of drops of jam on the ice-cold saucer. If it sets quickly and forms wrinkles when you push it with your finger, it is done. Otherwise, continue cooking for about 1 minute before repeating this test.

Stewed fruit tastes fabulous with Quark Dumplings (see p.138), Semolina Pudding (see p.199), or Kaiserschmarren (see p.154), but it is also wonderful eaten on its own or with yogurt.

Stewed Apricots

Makes 4 (9fl oz/250ml) jars

1kg ripe, juicy apricots
finely grated zest and juice of 1 organic lemon
½ vanilla bean
150–200g turbinado sugar (depending on the sweetness of the apricots)
50g water
50g clarified butter (ghee)
2 tbsp apricot brandy (optional)

Wash and halve the apricots. Remove the stones and put the fruit in a large saucepan. Add the lemon zest and juice. Slice the vanilla bean in half lengthwise, scrape out the seeds with a small, sharp knife, and add the seeds and bean to the apricots. Now add the sugar, mix everything together carefully, and let the flavors infuse for 30–45 minutes.

Add the water to the pan and heat. Stir in the clarified butter and apricot brandy, if using. Simmer over moderate heat for 10–15 minutes, stirring occasionally, until the fruit is soft. Depending on how ripe the apricots are, you may need to add more water.

Pour the fruit into sterilized jars while it is still hot, leaving ½ in of space at the top of the jar. Wipe the rim, seal with a canning lid, and process in boiling water for 10 minutes. Let the jam cool and check to ensure all of the lids sealed properly.

If stored in a cool dark place, the stewed apricots will keep for up to 6 months. After opening, store in the fridge and use within a few days.

The shelf life can be extended by adding more sugar. Clarified butter or ghee balances the acidity of the fruit.

Stewed Plums

Makes 4 (9fl oz/250ml) jars

1kg plums
360g granulated sugar
1 tsp citric acid
1 cinnamon stick
1 clove
200g water
1 tsp rum (optional)
2 tsp cornstarch

Wash, halve, pit, and then quarter the plums. Add the plums, sugar, citric acid, spices, water, and rum (if using) to a saucepan and heat. Simmer for about 5 minutes, stirring occasionally, until the skin on the plums begins to roll up.

Mix the cornstarch with some cold water and stir until smooth, then stir this into the stewed fruit. Cook the mixture down for 1–2 minutes until thick. Remove the cinnamon stick and clove, transfer the fruit into sterilized jars while it is still hot, leaving ½ in of space at the top of the jar. Wipe the rim, seal with a canning lid, and process in boiling water for 10 minutes. Let the jam cool and check to ensure all of the lids sealed properly.

If stored in a cool dark place, the stewed plums will keep for up to 1 year. After opening, store in the fridge and use within a few days.

Stewed Peaches

Makes 4 (9fl oz/250ml) jars

1kg ripe flavorful peaches
8g pectin
150–200g granulated sugar (depending on the sweetness of the peaches)
50g water
4 tsp peach brandy (optional)

Create a cross-shaped incision in the base of each peach. Bring a pan of water to a boil, put the peaches in a boiling water for 30 seconds, then remove and immerse in ice water before removing the skin. Drain well, slice in half, remove the stones, and chop into pieces.

Combine the pectin and sugar with the peaches and water in a large saucepan and slowly bring to a boil. Cook gently for about 10 minutes until the peaches are soft, stirring occasionally.

Add the peach brandy (if desired), then transfer the fruit into sterilized jars while it is still hot, leaving ½ in of space at the top of the jar. Wipe the rim, seal with a canning lid, and process in boiling water for 10 minutes. Let the jam cool and check to ensure all of the lids sealed properly.

If stored in a cool dark place, the stewed peaches will keep for up to 6 months. After opening, store in the fridge and use within a few days.

Gösser
Gösser Bierklinik
Gösser
Bierklinik

Index

D

E

F

G

H

Q

R

S

T

V

W

Y

About the Team

Bernadette Wörndl

RECIPES & FOOD STYLING

Bernadette is a cookbook author and food stylist from Vienna. She discovered food art while at the Vienna Art School, then gained experience in professional kitchens and worked for a period at Chez Panisse in San Francisco. When she isn't rustling up delicious items for cookbooks or magazines, she is a private chef, giving sourdough bread workshops and experimenting with wild ferments in her studio. The process of immersing herself in the world of early 20th century Viennese baking has brought her even closer to her native city.

www.bernadettewoerndl.at
Instagram: @bernadettewoerndl

Melina Kutelas

PHOTOGRAPHY

Melina Kutelas comes from Vienna and has Austrian-Greek roots. After finishing school, she moved to London, where she studied Fashion Styling & Design at the well-known Istituto Marangoni and worked as a fashion stylist. After returning to Vienna, she dedicated herself to the culinary world and in 2015 launched her blog *About that food.* Today she runs an acclaimed photo studio in Vienna, known for its creative staging of commercial and product photography and for cookbook design.

www.melinakutelas.com
Instagram: @melina.kutelas

Katharina Wind

EDITING, GERMAN EDITION

Katharina grew up in Germany and found a second home in Vienna more than 15 years ago. When editing, she allows the aroma of the words to pervade and imagines baking the recipes herself. She loves any kind of yeast dough and has now also come to love "sweet main courses."

Andrea Högerle

GRAPHICS AND TYPESETTING

Andrea moved to England while still a student. She returned with all sorts of ideas, and with her partner Simon Jefferson. The couple design cookbooks together with a combination of meticulous German attention to detail and a dash of English eccentricity.

www.jefferson-hoegerle.com

Author's Acknowledgments

Writing a book is never a solo project. Just like all the sweet recipes here, this book is made up of the finest ingredients, harmoniously coordinated and combined for maximum flavor. It comes alive through the people who do what they do with such incredible passion and flair.

Thanks to my project manager, Muriel Magon, for choosing me as the author for the wonderful subject of Viennese Bakery. Thank you for trusting this project to me and for giving me the freedom to work so independently on assembling this sweet concoction. Our collaboration has been like the cherry on a Punschkrapferl.

Thank you Melina, your photographs have created a feast for the eyes that rivals the skill of any baker. You have made every single dish as radiant as the citrus fruit grown at the Schönbrunn Palace.

Thank you Andrea, your artistic and harmonious design can be sensed on every page. The feeling this evokes rivals the enjoyment of sipping a Viennese coffee outdoors on a spring afternoon.

Thank you Katharina—a master baker of words—your finely tuned phrasing and your love of baking are worth their weight in gold. It was only with your assistance that every recipe reached its full potential.

Publisher's Acknowledgments

DK would like to thank Vanessa Bird for creating the index, Aditya Katyal for picture research, and Renee Wilmeth for US consulting.

Image credits

12 Getty Images: brandstaetter images / Hulton Archive / Imagno (top). **51 Alamy Stock Photo:** Lebrecht Music & Arts. **63 Alamy Stock Photo:** Lebrecht Music & Arts (top). **75 Getty Images:** brandstaetter images / Hulton Archive / Imagno. **119 Getty Images:** brandstaetter images / Hulton Archive / Imagno (right).

Translator Alison Tunley
Editor Kate Reeves-Brown

Editorial Director Cara Armstrong
Senior Editor Lucy Sienkowska
Senior US Editor Megan Douglass
Food and Drink Design Manager Tania Gomes
Pre-Production Designer Manish Upreti
Production Editor Pushpak Tyagi
Senior Production Controller
Stephanie McConnell
Art Director Maxine Pedliham
Publishing Director Stephanie Jackson

DK Verlag
Project support Muriel Magon
Production Sophie Schiela
Recipes, Text, and Food Styling Bernadette Wörndl
Original Recipes & Transcription Therese Schulz & Eva Scheiringer
Food and Mood Photography Melina Kutelas
Editor Katharina Wind
Graphic design Jefferson & Högerle

First American Edition, 2026
Published in the United States by DK Publishing, a division of Penguin Random House LLC
1745 Broadway, 20th Floor, New York, NY 10019

26 27 28 29 30 10 9 8 7 6 5 4 3 2 1
001–358055–Feb/2026

ISBN: 979-8-2173-0579-7

Printed and bound in China

www.dk.com

This book was made with Forest Stewardship Council™ certified paper—one small step in DK's commitment to a sustainable future.
Learn more at www.dk.com/uk/information/sustainability

NOTES:

The information and suggestions in this book have been carefully considered and checked by the author and publisher, however no guarantee is assumed. Neither the author nor the publisher and their representatives are liable for any personal, material, or financial damage.

Oven temperatures: Unless otherwise specified, oven temperatures refer to a bake setting. For convection ovens the temperature should be reduced by roughly 20°F. Consult the manufacturer's details for further information.

Stand mixer: A stand mixer was used to prepare some dishes in this book. If using a hand mixer, the mixing and kneading times should be adjusted accordingly.

Liquids: To ensure precise quantities, the liquid measurements have been given in grams.